HOSPITALITY
TO THE STRANGER

Dimensions of Moral Understanding

HOSPITALITY
TO THE STRANGER

THOMAS W. OGLETREE

FORTRESS PRESS   PHILADELPHIA

Library of Congress Cataloging in Publication Data

Ogletree, Thomas W.
  Hospitality to the stranger.

  Bibliography: p.
  Includes index.
  1. Christian ethics—Addresses, essays, lectures.
I. Title.
BJ1251.045 1985   241   84–18763
ISBN 0–8006–1839–4

1272H84   Printed in the United States of America   1–1839

In Memory of
Charles M. Prestwood, Jr.
1931—1977

CONTENTS

CONTENTS

CONTENTS

ACKNOWLEDGMENTS

This volume is a contribution to what I call fundamental ethics. Here I undertake to display some of the central constituents of the moral life and the manner of their appearing in concrete human experience. Most units of the volume were completed prior to the publication of *The Use of the Bible in Christian Ethics* (Philadelphia: Fortress Press, 1983). I would characterize them as preparatory studies to that volume. They elaborate preunderstandings of the moral life which are given with the structure of ordinary experience. These preunderstandings serve as hermeneutical guides in the explication and appropriation of traditional materials—especially the Bible—in constructive Christian ethics. They also enable us to incorporate studies of action in the human sciences into normative perspectives on the moral life.

Apart from the prologue and chapter 1, these studies have previously appeared as independent essays, though in contexts not widely available. Their publication in disparate times and places has concealed their systematic connections. Common strands in substance and method should become manifest when the reader examines them together.

In creating this volume, I have undertaken minor, largely stylistic revisions of the original studies. The notable exception is chapter 3, "The Relation of Values to Human Need." I have totally reconceived the last two sections of this chapter. The chapter sets forth a phenomenological approach to a general theory of values, suggesting the place in moral understanding of the value field as a whole. The intent of the revisions is to make explicit the role history plays in the realization of a coherent value set. Criticisms of readers and further reflections on selected phenomenological texts have led to a fresh rethinking of the themes central to the earlier draft. Chapter 1, "Fundamental Investigations in Christian Ethics," is altogether new. It places the studies in a larger systematic context, and elaborates some of their main themes. The "Prologue" unfolds features in the central metaphor—"Hospitality to the Stranger"—which stand behind the individual studies, bestowing on them a certain unity of perspective.

The title for the volume is taken from chapter 2. That study explicates systematically the implications for ethical theory of giving primacy to the presence of an "other" in our field of awareness. Ancient traditions of hospitality function as a metaphorical guide to the descriptive elaboration of the experience of otherness in moral understanding. The metaphor reappears in the discussion of a "hermeneutics of hospitality" in chapter 3. Otherwise, it remains implicit. Yet it does express a disposition which operates throughout. It can serve to characterize the ethical position which emerges in the volume as a whole.

"Hospitality to the Stranger: The Role of the "Other" in Moral Experience" was initially published in *Selected Papers, The American Society of Christian Ethics, Eighteenth Annual Meeting,* 1977. "The Relation of Values to Human Needs" appeared in the *Journal of the American Academy of Religion,* 45/1 Supplement (March, 1977). "The Activity of Interpreting in Moral Judgment" is reprinted from *The Journal of Religious Ethics,* 8/1 (Spring, 1980). "The Eschatological Horizon of New Testament Social Thought" appeared in *The Annual of the Society of Christian Ethics,* 1983. The original articles are copyrighted respectively by the Society of Christian Ethics, *Journal of the American Academy of Religion,* and *The Journal of Religious Ethics.* They are used by permission.

This volume is dedicated to the memory of my brother-in-law, Charles M. Prestwood, Jr. Dr. Prestwood was a creative teacher, a thoughtful scholar, and a faithful minister of the gospel. He combined in his ministry a love for the church and a passionate commitment to social justice. He was an unfailing source of encouragement as I first worked through the themes of these studies. His untimely death at the age of forty-six deprived me of one of my dearest friends and most honored colleagues. My sense of loss is shared by a multitude of his friends. It is borne with special acuteness by his widow, Bette, my sister, and his four daughters, Karen, Beverly, Donna, and Teresa, two of whom are following him in the church's ministry.

I wish to acknowledge the support of a cross-disciplinary grant from The Society for Values in Higher Education (1973–74) for the research underlying these studies. Successive summer grants from the Vanderbilt University Research Council (1975, 1976) facilitated my efforts to reduce the materials generated by my research to a form suitable for publication. I owe special thanks to John A. Hollar of Fortress Press, who offered valuable suggestions about the shape of the present volume.

Drew University   Thomas W. Ogletree
Madison, New Jersey

PROLOGUE:
HOSPITALITY TO THE STRANGER
AS METAPHOR FOR THE MORAL LIFE

You shall not oppress a stranger; you know the heart of a stranger, for you were strangers in the land of Egypt.

(Exod. 23:9)

Foxes have holes and birds of the air have nests, but the Son of man has nowhere to lay his head.

(Luke 9:58)

I was a stranger, and you welcomed me.

(Matt. 25:35)

The moral life is exceedingly rich and complex. It eludes our attempts to grasp its essential meaning in a single conception: the "golden mean," the disposition to do good and avoid evil, respect for law, the greatest happiness for the greatest number, fellow feeling, authentic existence, other regardingness. Nonetheless, we continually seek to devise and refine such conceptions in order that we might articulate more adequately the unity of moral experience. When successful, these conceptions direct our attention to important aspects of the moral life. At the same time, they invariably obscure other equally important aspects. They both sharpen and distort our comprehension, contributing to the ongoing dialectic of thought.

This volume is informed not so much by a single conception of morality as by an over-arching metaphor: to be moral is to be hospitable to the stranger. A metaphor involves seeing one thing in terms of another. This novel combination of meanings creates a semantic dissonance which shakes conventional notions and provokes a process of interpretation. As long as a metaphor is alive and continues to do its work, the dissonance it bears will

1

not yield to a definitive resolution. It contains indeterminate and ever unfolding dimensions of meaning, pressing the interpreter to retain an active imagination in the quest for understanding. Metaphor conveys a sense of the unity of experience while dramatizing its multi-faceted character.[1]

Despite their open-ended semantic structure, metaphors too are finite. They articulate what is given to awareness in a particular way. They bring into play a set of meanings which are interrelated, continually flowing into one another and activating one another. Though these meanings may be extraordinarily rich, they still cannot encompass all that we apprehend. They conceal even while they disclose. There is, Hans-Georg Gadamer observes, an infinity of the unsaid which always accompanies the finitude of the said.[2] A particular metaphor is never able to exhaust understanding, no matter how suggestive it may be. In fact, the more suggestive a metaphor is, the more it elicits other metaphors. Metaphor quickens rather than stifles the imagination.

For moral understanding, the central thrust of the metaphor of hospitality is to break the preoccupation of ethical theory with perceptions and reasonings stemming from a given actor's own vantage point on the world. It is to accomplish in ethics what Paul Ricoeur calls a "de-centering of perspective."[3] This emphasis is a corrective to the Western tendency to begin and end ethical analysis with a self—either logical or actual—who reads the experiences of others in terms of his or her own experiences, and who assimilates the moral import of the other into his or her own self-actualization. The metaphor forces us to recognize that the self's struggle to survive and to fulfill its own potential is not necessarily harmonious with the moral claims which others make upon it. Enjoyment and goodness are not always partners. Indeed, in the world as we know it, they are at best squabbling children, and at worst, mortal enemies.

To offer hospitality to a stranger is to welcome something new, unfamiliar, and unknown into our life-world. On the one hand, hospitality requires a recognition of the stranger's vulnerability in an alien social world. Strangers need shelter and sustenance in their travels, especially when they are moving through a hostile environment. On the other hand, hospitality designates occasions of potential discovery which can open up our narrow, provincial worlds. Strangers have stories to tell which we have never heard before, stories which can redirect our seeing and stimulate our imaginations. The stories invite us to view the world from a novel perspective. They display the finitude and relativity of our own orientation to meaning. The sharing of stories may prove threatening, but not necessarily so. It may generate a festive mood, a joy in celebrating the meeting of minds across social and cultural differences. The stranger does not simply challenge or subvert our assumed world of meaning; she may enrich, even transform, that world.

In its metaphorical usage, hospitality does not refer simply to literal instances of interactions with persons from societies and cultures other than our own. It suggests attention to "otherness" in its many expressions: wonder and awe in the presence of the holy, receptivity to unconscious impulses arising from our being as bodied selves, openness to the unfamiliar and unexpected in our most intimate relationships, regard for characteristic differences in the experiences of males and females, recognition of the role social location plays in molding perceptions and value orientations, efforts to transcend barriers generated by racial oppression. Human relations across culture and society are simply notable instances of a dynamic which runs through all aspects of moral experience: a readiness to honor what is "other" precisely in its "otherness." For theological ethics, the religious sense of otherness is foundational; the more proximate senses provide the material experience for apprehending the distinctive strangeness of the sacred. For moral understanding as such, relations between human "strangers" are in the center of attention.

Regard for strangers in their vulnerability and delight in their novel offerings presuppose that we perceive them as equals, as persons who share our common humanity in its myriad variations. Yet the concept of equality is too abstract to capture the specific dynamics which make up hospitality. Concrete interactions invariably have asymmetrical elements. When the stranger stands before me in his vulnerability, there is at least an inequality of power in our relationship. He has need of my recognition and service; I have at my disposal support systems which already suffice for my needs. I am "at home" in my world; he is in an unfamiliar place and does not know what to expect. However, when the stranger begins to tell her stories, a new kind of asymmetry appears. With regard to the world of meaning which she is uncovering, she enjoys a level of authority that wholly surpasses my own. I am the novice, she the expert. I can only sit at her feet to learn. That the stranger and I enjoy an equal dignity emerges concretely only as our interactions unfold over time.[4]

The equality of host and stranger finally shows itself in reciprocal acts of hospitality that reflect reversals in the relational order. My readiness to welcome the other into my world must be balanced by my readiness to enter the world of the other. My delight in the stories of the other as enrichment for my orientation to meaning must be matched by my willingness to allow my own stories to be incorporated into the values and thought modes of the other. What do my stories say when they are told in a strange household? The universal claims which are implicit in my perspective are offset by the universal claims residing in the perspective of the stranger. In short, the ramifications of hospitality are not fully manifest unless I also know the meaning of being a stranger.

Hospitality to the stranger points toward an ongoing dialectic of host and stranger. It expresses a fundamental recognition of the world's plurality. The point is not that I may have no world of my own, nor that my world is unworthy of vigorous defense and advocacy. It is that I can have my world in a moral way only as I learn to relate it positively to the contrasting worlds of others. The promise borne by the reciprocal dialectic of host and stranger is the emergence of a new world of shared meanings. We cannot predict or guarantee the accomplishment of such a world. Where it appears, it is a creation made possible by the productive imaginations of human beings. It requires for its formation persons and communities who have the patience to work out ways of being together as human beings which also show regard for differences. In the process, strangers may begin to feel more at home. They may even become friends, though the most intimate of friends can never be wholly transparent to one another.

Hospitality has relevance to the human assault on oppressive social structures, though its bearing on relations between oppressor and oppressed, or even between beneficiaries and victims of social oppression, is ambiguous. To be oppressed is to be virtually without a home. It is not only to be structurally vulnerable to those who wield power; it is also to be forced to work out a sense of self within a context determined by the definitions, priorities, and interests of the oppressor. One's own stories are continually recast and reassessed in the interpretations of the oppressor. They are changed into charming little playlets which offer comic relief within the great dramatic movement of reigning social stories. It is highly unlikely that persons who fare well in an oppressive social system will by themselves discover anything problematic about that system. The system will seem more or less "natural" and altogether inevitable. If anything new is to emerge, it will arise through the initiatives of the oppressed, assisted perhaps by a few class traitors.

For the oppressed, the moral imperative is not to display hospitality to strangers. The oppressed are daily subjected to an alien world quite against their wills. They are already forced to live in a society which denies them their full humanity. Their challenge is to secure social space within which an alternative world of meaning can be established and nurtured, generating resistance to oppression. It is to expose the deceit and the distortions of the dominant culture. It is to open the way for a new reading of social reality in the service of strategies directed toward social reformation.

In laboring to build up an alternative social world and in resisting taken-for-granted patterns in the existing order, people engage in a good deal of storytelling. The dynamic, however, is not that of a host entertaining and being entertained by a stranger. It is that of courageous people daring to share forbidden tales, bringing into view features of experience that have been suppressed if not altogether repressed. The listeners do not find strange or unfamiliar the stories they hear. They identify with them, seeing in them variants of their own stories. The stories disclose the fact that their private troubles have a social basis. The stories are freighted with intense emotion. They uncover deeply buried pain; they bring relief from fruitless acts of denial; they awaken joy in the discovery of companions who are one with them in suffering and struggle; they provoke rage over the irrationality and arbitrariness of the structures of oppression; they heighten a determination to resist to the uttermost any further humiliation and degradation.[5] Hospitality may eventually have a place in the moral life of those who have been oppressed, but only later and under quite different social circumstances.

Hospitality as a moral stance is more germane to beneficiaries of a system of oppression. There are always some individuals in any social order who are able to transcend the orientations to meaning which are given with their particular social locations. Such persons may become hospitable to the oppressed. They may recognize the profound vulnerability of the oppressed and respond to their suffering with compassion. Under certain circumstances they may even support the efforts of the oppressed to accomplish discrete social reforms. They may also open themselves to the stories of the oppressed, gaining a new understanding of social reality through what their stories unveil.

Yet under conditions of structural inequality, hospitality alone is an insufficient moral response to social oppression. In the stance of hospitality, the host continues to be "at home," which means he retains control. At most he only welcomes those who are socially estranged into his own world, and largely on the terms of that world. He cannot develop a reciprocal relation with the victims of oppression, for they have no world over which he does not already in some respects preside. He discovers that condescension and paternalism corrupt his hospitable intentions despite his conscious desire to avoid them. To be sure, he can surrender altogether the location which gives him power and privilege. If he does so, however, he will himself become a victim of oppression. He will have no further recourse than to move in solidarity with the oppressed toward the creation of a new world.

To become aware of oppressive features in a social system is to learn that something is profoundly wrong with that system, even when one experiences it as furnishing significant benefits. The appropriate response to a situation of oppression is not merely hospitality, but repentance, a deep turning of mind away from the familiar world toward the possibility of a new order of the world. In repentance one's former position of relative privilege is itself at risk. The old ways of being "at home" are acknowledged as morally bankrupt. One faces times of homelessness, a period of wandering in the wilderness, until the shape of things to come begins to appear. As a stance, hospitality can set in motion a movement of awareness which leads to repentance. When repentance occurs, however, the host-stranger dialectic gives way to solidarity in the struggle for liberation.

What complicates this account is the fact that oppressive social systems often contain elements of cultural pluralism as well. Those who differ in notable respects from dominant classes and groups tend to be relatively easy prey for subjugation and exploitation. Their strangeness is prima facie evidence that they do not fully share the humanity of those in control, and hence, are well suited for marginal social roles. Social and cultural pluralism are not necessarily dissolved, however, when particular structures of oppression are overcome. They may show themselves in surprisingly new ways. Ideally, the overcoming of social oppression will open the way to a genuine honoring of plurality, but things do not always work out that way. The fundamental point is that the host-stranger dialectic in its reciprocal expressions has pertinence to plurality among social equals. It is only obliquely and ambiguously relevant to situations of social and cultural oppression.

In the context of Christian eschatology the motif of hospitality takes on some additional nuances.[6] In the Pauline corpus and the Synoptic Gospels, the larger world within which people exist is itself portrayed as fundamentally alien. The world is under the dominion of evil and belongs to an age which is passing away. In the ministry of Jesus a new age is dawning which operates on fundamentally different principles. Followers of Jesus belong essentially to the new age even though they still carry on their lives in social contexts determined by the old. In the present age they are strangers in a strange and not particularly hospitable land. Their true home is beginning to take form in the world. They can know and taste its liberating power. Nonetheless, in considerable measure it is present to them only as promise. Even while participating in the life it brings, they must continue to endure in an alien land. In Jesus the God who establishes and sustains their true home has entered into the alien nature of their existence. He is himself a stranger, wholly vulnerable to a hostile, violent world. In welcoming him they discover that they too have been welcomed, received by grace as beloved of God.

Since the basis of their true home is no longer kinship or a common history and culture, but grace, they are less in need of familiar places and customs to stabilize their individual and corporate identities. They can become a pilgrim people, finding new companions in their life-journey from every race and nation and from every social stratum. They are summoned to community in which no particular manner of dwelling enjoys special privilege. The only requisite is that freedom be maintained and community fostered. In mutual recognition and with patience and forbearance they work toward new ways of being together which acknowledge and celebrate the world's plurality. Since all are strangers, no one is a stranger any more. Through their shared commitments, they are becoming sisters and brothers, the new family of God by faith.

Identity and plurality, the familiar and the strange, seeing through one's own eyes and seeing through the eyes of another, being at home in the world and being a pilgrim in a strange land, negotiating a common world and honoring plurality, welcoming strangers and venturing friendship with them, living with the dialectic of enjoyment and goodness—these are some of the motifs which come into play when traditions of hospitality guide our reflections on the nature of the moral life.

NOTES

1. Cf. Paul Ricoeur, *Interpretation Theory: Discourse and the Surplus of Meaning* (Fort Worth, Tex.: Texas Christian University Press, 1976), 49–53.

2. Hans-Georg Gadamer, *Truth and Method*, Eng. trans. by Garrett Barden and John Cumming (New York: Seabury Press, 1975), 416.

3. Paul Ricoeur, *Freedom and Nature: The Voluntary and the Involuntary*, Eng. trans. by Erazim V. Kohak (Evanston, Ill.: Northwestern University Press, 1966), 126.

4. I am indebted to the work of Immanual Levinas for this insight into the asymmetry of human interactions. Cf. his *Totality and Infinity: An Essay on Exteriority*, Eng. trans. by Alphonso Lingis (Pittsburgh: Duquesne University Press, 1969), 75.

5. Within feminist consciousness-raising processes, exchanges of this sort are referred to as the "yeah, yeah" experience. See Judith Plaskow, "The Coming of Lilith: Toward a Feminist Theology," in *Womanspirit Rising: A Feminist Reader in Religion*, eds. Carol Christ and Judith Plaskow (New York: Harper & Row, 1979), 200–201. I am indebted to my colleague Karen Brown for helping me grasp the ambiguity of the

hospitality metaphor as indicating an appropriate moral response to liberation thought.

6. The moral import of New Testament Eschatology is elaborated in chap. 5, "The Eschatological Horizon of New Testament Social Thought."

1

FUNDAMENTAL INVESTIGATIONS
IN CHRISTIAN ETHICS

Christian ethics can no longer be subsumed under one of the older theological disciplines, such as systematic theology or practical theology. It has become a relatively autonomous field of inquiry, drawing for its work upon a variety of disciplines, theological and non-theological. Even so, there is little scholarly consensus on what constitutes the field or on how its discrete inquires amount to one area of study. Undertaking work with systematic implications obliges us, therefore, to have in view a comprehensive conception of the field as a whole.

In this volume I assume three primary divisions to the field of Christian ethics: fundamental ethics, symbolic ethics, and practical ethics.[1] Fundamental ethics sets forth a basic account of the moral life. Its task is to identify the central subject matter of ethics. In so doing it furnishes a guide for critical investigations in the other divisions. It has two primary components. The most important is descriptive, a portrayal of the elemental constituents of the moral life and the manner of their appearing in concrete human experience. The aim of this portrayal is to show how moral understandings figure in the human way of being in the world. Phenomenological studies of the life-world provide its principal resources.[2]

The second component is constructive. It consists in the formulation of ethical theory. The intent of such theory is to articulate in a coherent and conceptually precise manner what is already given to awareness at a pre-reflective level. Theory attempts to represent in thought the totality of understanding which resides in human potentialities for being. It is never adequate to this totality since it always conceals as well as discloses, distorts as well as articulates. In considerable measure, moreover, theory is culture bound even though it embodies a mode of reasoning which is subject to a critical public discourse. Its function is to bestow greater conceptual clarity on what is already given to awareness in a specifiable region of experience.

Symbolic ethics critically interprets, appropriates, and mediates the traditions which give determinate character to our moral understandings. Here the theme is not the elemental constituents of our worldly being, but particular, historically relative configurations of shared meanings which mold, express, and bestow significance on the moral life of communities and societies to which we belong. The normative substance of distinctively Christian understandings comes to expression in symbolic ethics, though some of its contours are prefigured in a more general way in fundamental ethics. Symbolic ethics takes us into hermeneutics. It requires us to become reflective about what goes on in the activity of interpreting.

Practical ethics directs our attention to the conditioning and controlling factors which constrain and channel the moral life. Understanding these factors and their bearing on action is itself an important theoretical undertaking, especially given the contemporary importance of the human sciences. Practical ethics is not yet applied ethics, nor is it the locus of concrete moral guidance. Its task is to enlarge our grasp of the organic, psychic, social, and cultural dynamics operative in the moral life. These dynamics make up the systemic contexts of human life and activity. They can also be expanded to take account of the natural environment—its resources and limits. Indeed, the systemic factors in action have cosmological dimensions as well. They are founded on the final metaphysical facts which compose the structure of being as such.[3] Practical ethics enables us to examine our action possibilities in view of the systemic factors which condition and control human life processes.

The three divisions of Christian ethics comprise relatively independent yet essentially interconnected lines of inquiry. Each has its distinctive questions and its corresponding methods; yet each draws upon the others and is oriented to the others in carrying out its own proper tasks. None of the divisions finally enjoys primacy over the others, though there may be a certain convenience in an exposition which moves from fundamental to symbolic to practical ethics. The underlying basis for the distinct inquiries and for their interconnections is concrete experience itself: the everyday life-world as it presents itself to awareness.

THE DESCRIPTIVE TASK IN
FUNDAMENTAL ETHICS

Chapters 2, 3, and 4 in this volume address the descriptive task of fundamental ethics. They seek to delineate some of the more salient features in the moral understandings which are given with the life-world. The emphasis on description amounts to an implicit critique of much twentieth-century Anglo-American work in philosophical ethics. While that work has heightened our awareness of the peculiar logic of moral discourse, it has tended to obscure the experiential matrix which gives such discourse its significance. Either it deals only in passing with the way moral understandings come to awareness, or it reduces the experiential roots of moral understanding to purely subjective feeling.

This deficiency is already apparent in the two accounts of the moral life which have shaped most decisively the ethical perspectives of modern Anglo-American thought: Immanuel Kant's ethics of duty and British utilitarianism. Kant, for example, begins his account of ethics by setting forth what he takes to be the "moral knowledge of common human reason" and isolating its inner principle. This principle proves to be the "conception of law in itself," which the moral being is obliged to obey.[4] Having given "abstract and universal form" to what ordinary human beings already have "before their eyes,"[5] Kant commits himself to recasting this "popular moral philosophy" in a properly philosophic form, which he calls the metaphysic of morals.[6] His intent is to show not simply that morality, regard for duty, is philosophically possible—despite the deterministic thrust of the empirical sciences—but that it is logically entailed by the notion of practical reason. He examines the logic of the idea of a rational being, that is, a being who can determine himself to action on the basis of pure, practical reason alone, demonstrating that this idea not only supports a notion of morality, but that it founds morality as a necessary ingredient in practical reason as such.

It is not my purpose to examine the validity of Kant's argument, though I find it compelling. It is to note how quickly Kant moves from a characterization of our pre-reflective understandings of the moral life to their inner principle and then to a philosophical analysis which establishes the validity of that principle. He is quite confident that he has at the outset correctly identified the constitutive features of the moral life. In this respect his starting point is taken to be largely unproblematic. His philosophical argument serves in turn to confirm and reinforce his initial characterization, leaving it beyond critical examination.

Utilitarian thinkers place a good deal more weight on "experience" than Kant does. Indeed, in his own use of the term Kant rules experience out altogether as a resource for moral understanding.[7] In contrast, utilitarians build their ethical theories on a moral psychology. That psychology traces our notions of good and bad to elemental experiences of pleasure and pain. Jeremy Bentham's overly simple formula is a classic:

> Nature has placed mankind under the governance of two sovereign masters, *pain* and *pleasure*. It is for them alone to point out what we ought to do, as well as to determine what we shall do. On the one hand the standard of right and wrong, on the other the chain of causes and effects, are fastened to their throne.[8]

This equation, despite its surface attractions, has generated a plethora of difficult theoretical problems for ethics. Can one derive a notion of value from the experience of pleasure? Are "good" and "pleasurable" the same thing? Are all pleasures essentially alike, differing only in degree? Or do they differ qualitatively, disclosing qualitatively different kinds of values? And if values are qualitatively different, how are conflicts among discrete value claims to be adjudicated? How are heterogeneous values to be related and coherently ordered? Finally, is the experience of pleasure, and hence, the apprehension of value, essentially private and individual? Or is there a kind of social pleasure, a "fellow feeling," which binds us to other human beings? Stated differently, are we by nature egoists, requiring external sanctions to behave altruistically? Or are altruistic sentiments elemental features in our enjoyment of being?

Problems such as these have kept experiential aspects of the moral life in the forefront of utilitarian thought. Even so, the utilitarian tradition has not generated sustained descriptive studies of the ways in which moral understandings come to awareness in the everyday life-world. Rather, attempts to resolve analytic and conceptual problems at the theoretical level have been central. In general further attention to the descriptive undertaking has not appeared promising because of the dominance of empiricist assumptions in utilitarian conceptions of experience. As Kant saw clearly, these assumptions preclude the possibility of grasping the constitutive features of the moral life.

A central conviction informing the studies in this volume is that we need to attend with the greatest care to our pre-reflective understandings of the moral life before we move to theoretical constructions or to various forms of logical analysis and ethical argumentation. Indeed, our failure to do justice to this primal task has led us to create some puzzles and generate some contradictions that will not yield to a satisfactory resolution at a theoretical level.

The importance of phenomenology is that it gives us a productive new way of taking up the task of describing what is given in experience. "To the things themselves" is its leading idea. Indirectly, at least, this volume presents a case for the fruitfulness of phenomenology for deepening our awareness of the nature of the moral life. Chapter 2, "Hospitality to the Stranger: The Role of the 'Other' in Moral Experience," largely supports Kant's emphasis on duty. However, I do not link duty to the principle of law as such, but to the originality of the self's encounter with an "other." A notion of law is relevant to this encounter. Some of the preconditions for a meeting of selves can be stated in the form of moral laws or principles. Law can also set forth shared understandings, arising from the encounter, of the ground rules regulating ongoing relationships between the self and the other. Yet law is secondary to this encounter and dependent on it for its essential meaning. It is continually subject to revision in terms of the dynamics of concrete human interactions.

Chapter 3, "The Relation of Values to Human Needs," takes up some of the puzzles which have troubled the utilitarian tradition of ethical theory, particularly the relation of pleasure, need gratification, and the discernment of value. I seek to display the intricate connections of these phenomena without collapsing their discrete meanings. I also offer an account of the multiplicity of value modalities, and the possibilities of arriving at a relatively comprehensive and coherent value field. In effect I here challenge the formalist tendency to isolate the moral life from the total field of substantive human values. At the same time, I retain the formalist recognition of the primacy of our obligations to other selves. My intent is to increase our grasp of the density and complexity of the moral life. Fundamental ethics does not move us away from problems which have been central to philosophical and theological ethics. It takes up those problems in a new way, aided by the contributions of the phenomenological movement.

PHENOMENOLOGICAL CONTRIBUTIONS TO THE DESCRIPTIVE TASK

Phenomenology is based upon the discovery of intentionality. In this context intentionality refers to the orientation of consciousness to those meanings which make up its contents. It is not a term of purpose, as in our references to the intentions of moral actors. Rather, it identifies a basic structural relation between acts of consciousness and the materials of which we are conscious: objects, persons, dreams, fantasies, happenings. In Edmund Husserl's technical language, intentionality is a transcendental category; it points to a structural precondition for the appearance of anything whatever.[9] The task of phenomenology is to describe the constitutive features of the life-world in terms of the intentional structure of consciousness. This perspective entails making explicit the acts of consciousness which correspond to the various modalities of sense that present themselves to awareness in the life-world.

Phenomenological description is to be distinguished from empirical description. The latter generally discounts or disregards the peculiar nature of the acts of consciousness which figure in observation. It also gives privileged status to sense data, overlooking the degree of abstraction involved in their appearance. In contrast to a naive empiricism, phenomenology reminds us that we are not involved with our world in the first instance as bundles of sense data, but as concrete objects which serve or hinder our projects, as other selves who cooperate with us or frustrate us or make claims upon us, as a wider environment which sustains us in our being or leaves us helpless and vulnerable. To isolate sense data in awareness, we must suspend our concern-filled involvements with worldly realities, and take up an objectifying stance toward their sensory properties. Empirical descriptions are by no means illegitimate so long as their relative abstractness is kept in view. However, the primary interest of phenomenological description is the life-world itself and our everyday engagements in that world. It provides an account of the elemental structures which are the precondition of all experience whatever. These structures not only make up the life-world; they also found scientific and philosophical knowledge, or more generally, the full sweep of human cultural activity.

The seminal works in phenomenology have not been devoted primarily to ethics. Edmund Husserl was chiefly occupied with laying a philosophical foundation for the sciences, especially in view of revolutionary twentieth-century developments.[10] In keeping with this interest he gave primacy to epistemological problems. His studies of perception are especially noteworthy. He recognized the importance of value questions, but his own references to such matters were largely incidental. In fact, he tended, mistakenly I believe, to grant values a secondary and derivative status in the appearance of worldly realities. In contrast to Husserl's interest in the sciences, Martin Heidegger was seeking a way back into the question of the meaning of being.[11] This question, he contended, is the central philosophical question; but it has, unfortunately, largely been obscured in Western thought. To recover this question, Heidegger initially concentrated his attention on existential concerns, contending that it is in relation to these concerns that the question of the meaning of being appears. This question has bearing on moral understandings, especially for those who view the moral life in a religious frame of reference. Yet it does not in itself bring the moral life systematically into view.

When the moral life is the subject of investigation, three loci of inquiry emerge as central: action, patterned interactions (or social institutions), and the self as a moral being. These loci must then be examined against a larger meaning horizon, a horizon marked by the question of the meaning of being.

Action
Action is the starting point for inquiry since it marks the locus of origination in the moral life. Yet action always has direct ref-

erence to more or less stable patterns of social interaction, and indirect reference to the selfhood of the actor. It makes use of, sustains, or modifies existing patterns of social interaction; it expresses, confirms, expands, or perhaps disturbs and contradicts, the stabilities and habitualities which form the identity of the actor. Because of its potential for transcending these stable forms, action merits relatively independent treatment in ethical inquiry.

Action has two primary orientations: to the goals of the actor and to communicative interactions with other human beings. In the first, consciousness is directed toward projects which an actor is considering as a possibility for him- or herself. Here we have to do with intentions in the ordinary sense of that term. Projects bear value-type meanings, meanings which display and articulate for the actor the significance of the projects in view. These meanings are ingredient in the anticipated outcomes of action. Accounts of goal-oriented actions, including the processes of deciding upon a course of action, lead us to studies of values and the manner of their appearing in the life-world. They suggest the importance of a general theory of values in moral understanding. This set of problems is the focus of attention in chapter 3, "The Relation of Values to Human Needs." Of special interest here is a consideration of embodiment and its role in the discernment of value.

In communicative interactions, consciousness is not oriented to projects, but to the appearance of an "other" in a field of awareness. The other is one who, like me, is a center of orientation onto the world and its meanings. As a valuing being the other presents him- or herself as a privileged locus of value, one not to be violated or simply used. In this respect, the other sets limits to morally permissible projects. I cannot violate or use the other unless I have first apprehended that other as suitable material for use, or perhaps abuse. In communicative interactions the other also makes claims upon me, claims for my loyalty and service. The claims have their basis in the distinctive being of the other as a center of valuation toward the world. Yet they are reinforced and undergirded by my discovery that the other's regard for me and loyalty and service to me are conditions of my own being, my existing, and my flourishing. These exchanges are the subject matter of chapter 2, "Hospitality to the Stranger: The Role of the 'Other' in Moral Experience."

Communicative interactions are not strictly speaking goal-oriented. I may participate in them and take account of them in order to further my projects; and they may issue in collective projects where individual actors coordinate their diverse acts to achieve common goals. In themselves, however, they do not concern goals. They concern gestures in which two or more persons reach toward shared understandings. In the process, a common world emerges. Human community is nascent in attempts to communicate, and the maturation of community facilitates fuller and richer communication. The break-down of communication leads to a reverse movement, a vicious circle in which enmity and alienation intensify misunderstanding, undermining the bases for community.

The limits and claims called forth by the presence of the other imply stable patterns of obligation, negative and positive duties which not only set the conditions for successful communication but also intersect our projects. With regard to our projects, these duties function as regulative principles of action. They constrain our actions in certain ways, whatever our goals may be. They specify the appropriate manner of pursuing our goals. With reference to communicative interactions, the duties are constitutive. They set the requisite conditions for communication and also express any consensus about human order which may have been gained through communication. These duties, and the values they serve, make up the central content of the moral law. In this respect, it is proper to speak of morality as consisting in "other regardingness." The biblical image of "hospitality to the stranger" provides a dramatic metaphor of moral receptivity to an "other." Yet moral values always appear against the background of the total field of values: sensible, organic, psychic, social, cultural, religious. Likewise, communicative interactions take place in relation to goal-oriented actions. Both sorts of actions and their relationships belong to an account of the moral life. Following the suggestion of Immanuel Levinas, I speak of the relation between moral and nonmoral values in terms of a dialectic between goodness and enjoyment.

Chapter 4, "The Activity of Interpreting in Moral Judgment," also deals with communicative interactions, but now in a fashion that makes explicit the temporal horizon of experience. Human interactions do not occur in a vacuum, but in a social and cultural context stamped by a more or less extended history. That history bears powerful prejudices which both give us access to worldly realities and conceal those realities. These prejudices are our taken-for-granted ideas and assumptions about how things are and what they ought to be. They structure our perceptions and our interactions until something occurs to place them in question. This account builds upon H. Richard Niebuhr's contention that the first question in ethics is "What is going on?" It sets forth the possibilities in human interactions for uncovering prejudices which prevent us from grasping in a morally appropriate way "what is going on." It also suggests how we might negotiate new, shared understandings which disclose more adequately our concrete human reality. This chapter supplements the more abstract account of self-other interactions in chapter 2, "Hospitality to the Stranger."

Patterned Interactions

In this volume I do not give systematic attention to patterned interactions or to the moral actor, though these areas of investigation are viewed as crucial components of the descriptive work of fundamental ethics.[12] A brief sketch of their central features is in order.

Action always presupposes and involves a social world. In coming to consciousness of my action possibilities, I find myself already in a social world ordered by shared expectations about how typical kinds of actors are to act in typical situations. These shared expectations create ordered space for human action. They define appropriate, permissible, and obligatory patterns of action. Action is itself directed in no small measure toward the maintenance of social order. It has an institutional reference. A phenomenology of the social world describes the operation of typified expectations in institutional life and displays their role in action.[13] It seeks to show how social institutions present themselves in the everyday life-world.

In the life-world, institutional arrangements do not ordinarily manifest themselves as contingent, historically relative human constructions.[14] They appear rather as features in the stable realities we confront in acting. They provide the social matrix of action, effectively defining its limits and open possibilities. Under these circumstances, questions concerning the nature and the desired shape of social institutions are not likely to emerge as themes for moral reflection. Institutions are simply a feature in the experienced necessities of life. They may present problems for "consent" (Paul Ricoeur), but not for choice. That is, insofar as they evoke an evaluative language, that language will more likely set forth a theodicy explaining their necessity than criteria to assess their special merits alongside of alternative possibilities for social order.[15] Consequently, it should not be surprising that many treatments of ethics, both classical and modern, largely ignore institutions except insofar as they make up the framework within which action occurs, or perhaps indicate a social need for persons having particular gifts and strengths. Institutions are taken as givens to be understood, tolerated, defended, perhaps gratefully accepted, but certainly endured, for better or worse.

In contrast, consciousness of the constructed nature of social institutions awakens normative reflection on their desired shape and character. It leads to investigations of the duties likely to be generated by various kinds of social arrangements, and of the values favored by them. It calls forth consideration of ways to reform or reorder institutionalized patterns of social life. Rather than simply structuring our action possibilities, institutions themselves become objects for goal-oriented actions and occasions for communicative interactions. Notions of human community which are latent in communicative interactions suggest general norms for the direction of institutional change. The question is this: what patterned arrangements will tend to further communicative interactions and the forms of communal life they make possible? What arrangements will best protect and serve human life, dignity, and well-being?[16]

We do well not to oversimplify the senses in which social institutions are human constructions. Even in times of rapid change, institution-building and institutional reform are by no means fully subject to purposive direction. Social institutions are made up of highly complex, widely dispersed processes, most of which escape our awareness and control. Moreover, the most sweeping social changes depend heavily for their realization on regions of stability and an already existing stock of knowledge.

Institutionalized processes continually take on a life of their own. If we are to gain a measure of control over their central dynamics, we have to abandon the "natural attitude" of the life-world and take up the vantage point of the sciences. Attention to matters brought into view by way of this vantage point takes us out of fundamental ethics and into practical ethics. Nonetheless, a consideration of institutional arrangements, their aptness for human life and well-being, is at least a latent task for moral understanding in the everyday life-world. It is that level of awareness that fundamental ethics seeks to bring into view.

Actors

Action not only presupposes a stable social world; it also presupposes an actor. In deciding upon a course of action, I give expression to who I am; no less important, I also decide who I shall be. Action has a reflexive thrust, implicating the actor's being in the action itself.[17]

Phenomenology calls attention to the difficulty of making the being of the actor a theme.[18] Though phenomenology investigates consciousness and its contents, it is not as such a psychology. Its starting point is the "natural attitude" which characterizes our everyday worldly involvements. In this attitude consciousness is oriented in the first instance to projects or to other actors or to typifications which define the social world. In acting we are only indirectly aware of ourselves, and then only insofar as our being as selves is implicated in our acts. To become conscious of ourselves, we must make a reflexive turn in awareness. We must provisionally suspend our ongoing worldly involvements and consider retrospectively who we have been in our previous actions and who we will have become should we adopt particular action possibilities in the future. Even in the reflexive move we cannot bring ourselves before consciousness in "vivid immediacy" (Alfred Schutz), that is, as actively engaged in the world.[19] We cannot see ourselves as others see us. We can only manage the backward glance, reflecting on the import of completed deeds, actual or imagined. What we apprehend is the self as already formed, the sedimented, stabilized self, not the self moving into an open future with not-yet-realized potentialities. Moreover, we only grasp the self insofar as it appears to consciousness, not the unconscious dynamics which continually surprise us and catch us off our guard.

21

This retrospective glance does, nonetheless, enable us to uncover the bases of action in the stabilities and continuities of the self. These stabilities and continuities provide us with both the capacities to act and the resources to assess our actions. In traditional moral language capacities and resources of this sort are called virtues, those strengths and excellencies of character which perfect our powers. Their reference is to the being of actors, not to action as such, nor to the institutions which provide the context of action.

In classical moral theory attempts have been made to account for the formation of virtues, for example, as in the Aristotelian contention that we become habituated to virtue by acting well. Yet theories of formation lie beyond the reach of fundamental ethics. Fundamental ethics centers in description. It can set forth the ways in which virtues appear to awareness, and the kinds of "meanings" that compose them. It cannot explain their emergence nor suggest strategies for developing them. For the latter inquiries, we require here as well the objectifying perspectives of the sciences, especially developmental psychology. Working with theoretical models, these sciences project hypotheses about the dynamics at work in human development and subject those hypotheses to appropriate empirical tests. Procedures of this sort are essential if we are to have something more than merely common sense knowledge of human growth. Nonetheless, the phenomenological approach remains crucial if we are to sustain a moral perspective on the dynamics of growth. It keeps our attention oriented to the concrete experiences which bear to us an awareness of our beings as moral actors.

The Question of the Meaning of Being

One can deal with the discrete meanings that make up specifically moral understandings without moving explicitly to the final horizon of meaning which unfolds before them. In many contexts, the presence of that horizon can and doubtless will be left unnoticed and unnamed. Under those circumstances our everyday, practical engagements occupy us almost exclusively. Nonetheless, an ultimate horizon of meaning does hover before these engagements, at least as a question, a possibility; this horizon belongs inextricably to that totality of understanding which is the distinctive promise and threat of the human way of being in the world. It holds special importance for treatments of ethics which self-consciously attend to religious dimensions of moral understanding. Without some sense of its significance, of the questions it poses for our existence, we cannot satisfactorily articulate all that is going on in the moral life.

Within the phenomenological movement, Martin Heidegger has been the primary guide for reflection on this dimension of understanding. As noted earlier, he identifies the question of the meaning of being as the central subject matter of phenomenology properly conceived.

What is the question of the meaning of being, and how does that question show itself in the life-world? A direct answer is not possible, for we can speak of this question only in terms of its appearance to us as human beings. Human beings are, however, those beings for whom the question of being is a meaningful question. In Heidegger's language, we are the "being-there" (*Dasein*) of "being" (*Sein*). For human awareness, the appearance of the question of the meaning of being is linked to the recognition and acceptance of finitude. Heidegger focuses his attention on the way in which our orientation to death discloses to us our finitude. We are beings who can anticipate our own deaths, and who must, therefore, incorporate them positively into our living if we are to realize our distinctive potential. More broadly, our finitude means that we are beings marked by "care."[20]

Care bears the sense of anxious care. It reflects our struggle for survival, for a sense of self, for recognition and standing with our fellow human beings. Insofar as care is anxious, it continually drives us to avoid the import of our finitude: by immersing ourselves in everyday activities, by conventionality and triviality, by self-deceptive moves of various sorts. In all of these ways we conceal from ourselves the question of the meaning of being, and in the process truncate our humanity as well. Yet care also bears a more fundamental possibility. Here the prominent connotations of the word involve senses of "caring for." Care then suggests tending to, cultivating, nurturing: caring for the earth and what it gives forth as opposed to merely exploiting it; being "for" our fellow human beings as opposed to merely pleasing them or condescendingly "taking care of" them, and certainly in contrast to using or violating them. We are set free to care in this nurturing sense when and insofar as we acknowledge and accept our finitude, receive it, Heidegger says, as gift, as grace.[21]

The recognition and acceptance of finitude does not in Heidegger's reading result in the total dissolution of anxious care. It rather includes an acknowledgement of the persistent and inevitable recurrence of anxious care. Care never loses its double sense: anxiety and solicitude. Both meanings belong to the kinds of beings we are. This dual possibility is in a sense our fate since we cannot finally escape it; but we continually discover ourselves to be accomplices in acting it out. Openness to the meaning of being involves not only accepting our finitude in the neutral sense of limitation, an acceptance which frees us to realize the potentialities which are genuinely ours; it involves as well a readiness to "become guilty" for our active complicity in our recurring flight from finitude, that is, to "own" the fact that our avoidance of being is a feature of our being. Only by fully embracing the ambiguity of our existence are we free to "dwell" in the earth. Dwelling involves a receptivity to the question of the meaning of being in this radical and thoroughgoing sense.[22]

This account, though not itself specifically religious, prepares us to attend to the import of religious understandings for the moral life. Religious understandings are borne by concrete religious phenomena: symbolic representations of the sacred, sacred occasions and sacred places, spirit-filled persons, socially shared rituals and patterns of piety, myths recounting world origins, explanations of the human plight, annunications of the way to deliverance. Interpreting the content of such phenomena is the province of symbolic ethics. Yet fundamental ethics can uncover those modalities of awareness in the everyday life-world which display human receptivity to explicit religious understandings and involvements. Fundamental ethics can also guide us in thinking through the complex relationships which link moral and religious understandings to each other. In both respects it prepares for and contributes to symbolic ethics.

This sketch designates the studies which are primary for the descriptive side of fundamental ethics. Fundamental ethics undertakes to provide descriptions of action, patterned interactions, and human actors in terms of their significance for moral understanding. Moral understanding is then itself examined in relation to the horizon of meaning which is opened up by the question of the meaning of being.

THE CONSTRUCTIVE TASK IN
FUNDAMENTAL ETHICS

Fundamental ethics also has a constructive task, the conceptual articulation of moral understandings already given to awareness at a pre-reflective level. This constructive task can be characterized, with Kant, as an attempt to isolate the inner principles of the "moral knowledge of common human reason." It proceeds from the everyday life-world and moves to philosophical analysis and construction. Its purpose is to give us a firmer critical grasp of what is already available to understanding. Its criteria are clarity, precision, logical consistency and coherence, and, of course, fidelity to what is pre-reflectively present in awareness.

No theory can do full justice to the totality of what is understood. It can only give expression to certain aspects of that totality, ideally those most pertinent to a particular social and cultural setting. Every theoretical formulation conceals as well as reveals, and the concealment reflects not simply the finitude of perspective but motivated distortions and misrepresentations stemming from vested interests. Consequently, ethical theories must be continually subject to criticism, not simply for the sake of greater clarity and coherence, but to test the adequacy of their underlying assumptions and controlling images for comprehending concrete social realities.

Constructive aspects of fundamental ethics are evident throughout this volume, especially in the work of criticism. At no point, however, is the constructive undertaking given systematic development. To illustrate what is involved, I would refer the reader to my article on "Values, Obligations and Virtues: Approaches to Bio-Medical Ethics."[23] This article highlights some of the practical implications of three theoretical orientations currently dominant in the literature of philosophical and religious ethics. The method used in examining these orientations is logical-analytical. Three questions are central: What is the inner principle of each orientation? What are the sources of the various principles in the life-world? What is entailed by these principles in the assessment of moral problems generated by a particular area of current biomedical research?

Yet the interest of the article is not simply analytical but constructive. It searches for ways of adjudicating disputes among the major orientations, chiefly by suggesting a more comprehensive theoretical framework which gives to each its due. The move toward synthesis is called forth by a prior judgment, namely, that any theoretical orientation in ethics derives its legitimacy and significance from its ability to articulate what is already given to awareness at a pre-reflective level. The suggestion is made that the approaches to ethics under review enjoy their persistence and their persuasiveness because of their rootage in certain aspects of moral understanding which are integral to the basic constituents of the life-world. Theories which give primacy to our obligations to other human beings stem from understandings disclosed in communicative interactions. Theories which stress the consequences of our deeds and the values likely to be promoted by various action alternatives arise from understandings lodged in goal-oriented actions. Theories which accent virtues emerge from understandings generated by the concrete historicity of situations of choice, supported by a general awareness of the importance of the being of the actor in moral judgment and action. Since each of the structures cited belongs to the life-world, it is reasonable to suppose that the understandings they generate all have a legitimate place in a constructive ethical theory. The problem is to formulate the relevant theoretical elements in a fashion which suggests their interconnections and enables us to relate them coherently to one another.

These suggestions are no more than fragments of the theoretical task. They are linked almost exclusively to the first locus of inquiry cited above, namely, action and the norms which govern it. And the theoretical framework proposed for integrating the major approaches to the moral assessment of action is far from complete.

In *The Use of the Bible in Christian Ethics* I have attempted to move this discussion one step further. Instead of speaking of "obligation dominant," "value dominant," and "virtue dominant" perspectives, I use the more familiar categories: deontological, consequentialist, and perfectionist perspectives. I suggest that the inner connection of these perspectives is best seen by way of a fourth perspective which, following Gibson Winter, I call historical contextualism.[24] The discussion in chapter 4 of this volume, "The Activity of Interpreting in Moral Judgment," is governed by historical contextualism. Essentially this perspective associates the unity of moral understanding with the temporal horizon of the life-world. Since temporality structures goal-oriented actions, communicative interactions, and the continuities and stabilities of the moral actor, it discloses the concrete meaning of the major theoretical orientations and also their concrete interactions in moral awareness. Because of its centrality to these processes, temporality offers the most promising way into a more encompassing ethical theory. Such a theory will not remove the conflicts and strains which are reflected in competing ethical theories, for they are integral features of the moral life itself. Such conflicts cannot be overcome at a purely conceptual level. They must be lived through in the quest for moral wisdom and in the struggle for moral power. A more complex and embracing theory will, however, increase our understanding of these conflicts and strains, enabling us to deal with them more critically.

Since ethical theory builds upon the descriptive accomplishments of fundamental ethics, its systematic development is organized around the loci of inquiry already noted: action, patterned interactions, and the being of actors. Where action is the theme, the most difficult problems concern the articulation of a general theory of values and the clarification of the relation of the field of values, taken as a whole, to moral understandings. Such a theory would enable us to resist the tendency of consequentialist ethical thought to reduce the value realm to economic goods and services and to expressed political preferences. It would also heighten our appreciation for the density of moral experience. Similarly, we have need of more adequate accounts of the status of principles and rules (moral law) in the guidance of action. In particular we need to learn how to interpret those principles and rules with sensitivity to the concrete meanings they bear in particular social and cultural contexts.[25]

The controversies having the most far-reaching consequences are those concerned with the institutional settings of action. I have not yet given sufficient attention at a theoretical level to the complex organizations and social arrangements which order human life in post-industrial society. How ought traditional notions of office and calling, or of citizenship in the polis, be reformulated to establish closer contact with the actual life situations of contemporary human beings? The most explosive issues relate, however, to the ethical analysis and criticism of social structures in contemporary societies: advanced capitalist societies, emerging socialist societies, the state capitalism of the Soviet Union and of Eastern Europe, the oligarchic organization of global capitalism in third-world societies. What theoretical framework might facilitate such criticism? How might we take account in our ethical analysis of the different organizational principles that structure various types of societies? These questions gain their full meaning only when the contributions of practical ethics are also in view.

Where studies of agency are under consideration, the primary tasks requiring attention concern the fuller integration of accounts of temporality and embodiment into presentations of those strengths and competencies we call virtues. No less important is the maintenance of a clear sense of the sociality of the self in portraying actors as centered moral beings. The recovery of interest in notions of character is quite important in current ethical discussions, yet the possible contributions of phenomenology to those discussions are only in the early stages of formulation. Finally, theories of agency require a more satisfactory indication of the place which social-psychological perspectives on moral development might have in our total understanding. Here too we are moving to an inquiry which involves us in practical ethics.

THE CONTRIBUTIONS OF
FUNDAMENTAL ETHICS TO SYMBOLIC
AND PRACTICAL ETHICS

In the initial account of the three divisions of ethical inquiry, I emphasized their interdependence. An adequate demonstration of that interdependence awaits further developments in the work of the divisions. Yet some statement of the contributions of fundamental ethics to the remaining divisions may help to display the import of studies such as those contained in this volume.

With reference to symbolic ethics, the task of fundamental ethics is to make explicit the preunderstandings which guide our retrieval, criticism, and appropriation of the traditions which give determinate shape to Christian ethics. What complicates this undertaking is the fact that the major strands of Christian tradition are already formative elements in our pre-understandings. Moreover, these strands are for the most part effective in contemporary awareness in forms that are domesticated, truncated, and distorted. They are also mixed with alien materials, only some of which are finally compatible with their essential thrust. The aim of interpretation is to sort out these various elements, to identify the central impulses of the tradition, and to display their promise for contemporary understandings.

The motivation for taking up the work of interpretation is provided by a sense of problem, an awareness of difficulty, in our taken-for-granted understandings. Interpreting, Hans-Georg Gadamer notes, presupposes a "region of ignorance" which disturbs us, leaving us dissatisfied with conventional notions already at our disposal.[26] We re-read classical texts and reexamine the traditions they bear only when we are open to the possibility that they have something to teach us which we do not yet know. Our pre-understandings cannot, therefore, be permitted to control what we find in the texts. Indeed, where the pre-understandings do in fact control our interpretations, we are not engaging the tradition at all. We are merely employing its sanctity to reinforce and perhaps legitimate our own prejudices. Rather than serving as a source of illumination, tradition then functions as ideological cover to conceal or divert attention from the realities of our world. The pre-understandings which guide our inquiry must ever be subject to questioning, to transformation, as a result of a genuine conversation with the texts. Their function is to help us identify the subject matter which interests us as we take up a serious reading of the texts. The goal of interpretation is the realization of common ground with the texts, a fresh understanding of that about which the texts speak in unity with our own best critical grasp of what is morally at stake in our own situation. This common ground is the normative center of Christian ethics, incorporating the contributions of fundamental ethics and taking account of the results of practical ethics.[27]

Only chapter 5 of this volume, "The Eschatological Horizon of New Testament Social Thought," embodies the inquiries which belong to symbolic ethics. Here I do not move fully into the systematic task of symbolic ethics. This is preparatory work to such an undertaking, the first attempt at a retrieval of New

Testament traditions. Yet I do take into account the central challenge for a constructive Christian ethics, namely, interpreting the import of New Testament eschatology for moral understanding. In this respect, chapter 5 may have suggestiveness beyond its own accomplishment.

Fundamental ethics serves practical ethics by equipping it to maintain the primacy of moral understandings in making use of scientific perspectives on human life. The human sciences surface the conditioning and controlling factors which figure in human existence. Understanding these factors and their role in the moral life is a vital part of critical ethical thinking. The problem is that many students of human action mistakenly assume that the methods and categories of the sciences provide us with privileged access to concrete reality. In comparison moral understandings are often viewed as inconsequential subjective accompaniments of actual life processes. Phenomenology enables us to see the abstractness of the human sciences and to recognize their essential dependence on the constitutive structures of the everyday life-world. In so doing, it permits us to give due weight to scientific knowledge without losing our hold on the primary place of moral understandings in human activity.

Practical ethics is not concerned simply with the placement of human science perspectives in the totality of human understanding. It is also engaged in an ethical critique of the sciences. Differences among scientific theories or even particular scientific studies are not merely of scientific interest. These differences involve ethical questions as well. The processes of defining appropriate research subjects and of devising ways to get at them are never morally neutral. They are invariably energized by interests and concerns which bear morally important considerations. It is the business of practical ethics to call attention to these moral considerations and to assess them with the aid of the normative thinking generated by fundamental and symbolic ethics. This task complements the prior interest in isolating the realistic possibilities of action which are brought into view by the human sciences. The normative assessment of the sciences is itself aided by the critical consciousness of scholars specializing in the human sciences.

The systematic development of Christian ethics as a field of inquiry is a complex and many-faceted undertaking, one which surpasses the capacities of any single person. My work in this volume aims to advance that development in ways which have not yet received the attention they deserve.

NOTES

1. These categories are adapted from David Tracy's account of the "three disciplines" in theology: fundamental, systematic, and practical. Tracy is identifying basic types of theology, though his own perspective is a synthesis of the three. He locates ethical questions in practical theology. I am contending that ethical studies pose original lines of inquiry in fundamental and symbolic divisions as well, and I am emphasizing the theoretical character of practical ethics as opposed to applied ethics or practical moral guidance. With Tracy, I stress the essential interconnections of the three divisions. Cf. *The Analogical Imagination: Christian Theology and the Culture of Pluralism* (New York: Crossroad, 1981), 54–79.

2. There are alternative ways of addressing more or less equivalent questions. Perspectives which draw upon the philosophies of language in analyzing moral discourse take up similar matters under the rubric of metaethics. Yet fundamental ethics gives a primacy to concrete experience which is different in basic thrust than an account of the peculiar logic of moral utterances.

3. In these formulations I am guided chiefly by Talcott Parsons' account of the major facets of a general theory of action. See, e.g., his table of the sub-systems of action in the essay, "The Concept of Society: The Components and their Interrelations," in *Politics and Social Structure* (New York: Free Press, 1969), 32. For the fuller exposition, see especially pp. 5–8, 11–18. Gibson Winter's *Elements for a Social Ethic: Scientific and Ethical Perspectives on Social Process* (New York: MacMillan Co., 1966) is the most sustained treatment of practical ethics to appear thus far.

4. Immanuel Kant, *Fundamental Principles of the Metaphysic of Morals*, Eng. trans. Thomas K. Abbott (Indianapolis, Ind.: Bobbs-Merrill, Library of Liberal Arts, 1949), 19.

5. Ibid., 21.

6. Ibid., 27–28.

7. Ibid., 24–25.

8. Jeremy Bentham, *An Introduction to the Principles of Morals and Legislation* (1789), reprinted in *The English Philosophers from Bacon to Mill*, ed. Edwin A. Burtt (New York: Modern Library, 1939), 791.

9. Edmund Husserl, *The Crisis of European Sciences and Transcendental Phenomenology: An Introduction to Phenomenological Philos-*

ophy, Eng. trans. with an intro. by David Carr (Evanston, Ill.: Northwestern University Press, 1970), 165–67.

10. Ibid., 3–18.

11. Martin Heidegger, *Being and Time*, Eng. trans. John Macquarrie and Edward Robinson (London: SCM Press, 1962), esp. 21–35.

12. In considerable measure Howard L. Harrod's recent study, *The Human Center: Moral Agency in the Social World* (Philadelphia: Fortress Press, 1981), supplements my studies of action. My work differs chiefly in the fact that I stress more than he the need for a relatively independent treatment of action. Harrod largely incorporates the consideration of action into accounts of moral agency and patterned interactions (the social world as composed of institutional structures). Also, Harrod has not yet spelled out the import of his work for more familiar theoretical problems in contemporary philosophical and theological ethics. His interest is oriented primarily to the sociology of religion.

13. The work of Alfred Schutz provides the key resource for these investigations. See his *Collected Papers*, vol. 1, *The Problem of Social Reality* (The Hague: Martinus Nijhoff, 1967). See also Alfred Schutz and Thomas Luckmann, *The Structures of the Life-World*, Eng. trans. Richard M. Zaner and H. Tristram Engelhardt, Jr. (Evanston, Ill.: Northwestern University Press, 1973). Schutz has had special interest in the philosophical status of the social sciences, providing studies which compare the orientations of the everyday life-world with those of the social sciences. He calls attention to the essential dependence of the latter on the former. His work is especially important for practical ethics, as has been demonstrated in Gibson Winter's *Elements for a Social Ethic*.

14. For a helpful treatment of the "constructed" nature of the social world, see Peter L. Berger and Thomas Luckmann, *The Social Construction of Reality: A Treatise in the Sociology of Knowledge* (New York: Doubleday & Co., Anchor Books, 1967). The Berger-Luckmann volume draws heavily on the prior accomplishments of Alfred Schutz.

15. For Ricoeur's treatment of the concept of consent, see his *Freedom and Nature*, 341–54, 444–81. I discuss this motif in chap. 3, "The Relation of Values to Human Need."

16. Jürgen Habermas exemplifies these moves in his critical writings. Compare especially the essay, "What is Universal Pragmatics?" in *Communication and the Evolution of Society*, Eng. trans. Thomas McCarthy (Boston: Beacon Press, 1976), 1–68, and the monograph, *Legitimation Crisis*, Eng. trans. Thomas McCarthy (Boston: Beacon Press, 1973). "Universal Pragmatics" is about the universal conditions of practical action, and practical action is understood as communicative interaction among human beings. In Habermas's account these universal conditions are chiefly moral. They specify the basic requisites of human communication. Habermas's conceptions of these requisites lie in the back-

ground of his critical analysis of advanced capitalist society. In *Legitimation Crisis*, the burden of the critique is system-analytical rather than ethical. The question is this: what are the points of systemic vulnerability in advanced capitalist societies which indicate how dynamics leading to fundamental social change might get underway? The conditioning and controlling factors in social action are in the forefront of attention. This question is, however, energized at every point by an ethical interest. The work has direct relevance for practical ethics .

17. See Ricoeur, *Freedom and Nature*, 55–65.

18. Husserl in particular accents the difference between transcendental phenomenology and phenomenological psychology. Cf. *The Crisis of European Sciences and Transcendental Phenomenology*, 198–215. The most influential treatments of the self within phenomenology have had a therapeutic rather than an ethical interest. One might call to mind, however, Jean Nabert's *Elements for an Ethic*, Eng. trans. William J. Petrek (Evanston, Ill.: Northwestern University Press, 1969). Nabert's work is not, strictly speaking, phenomenological. It stands in the tradition of French reflexive philosophy. Still, it has affinities with the understanding of fundamental ethics here being advocated. Nabert identifies ethics with reflection on the self's "desire and struggle to exist." This association gives primacy to the self-constitution of the moral agent in contrast to my emphasis on the orientation of moral awareness to the "other."

19. Cf. Schutz, *Collected Papers*, I:172–75.

20. Heidegger, *Being and Time*, 225–73. Cf. also Martin Heidegger, "Letter on Humanism," in *Philosophy in the Twentieth Century: An Anthology*, ed. William Barrett and Henry D. Aiken (New York: Random House, 1962), 3:282, 285, 293–94; and Martin Heidegger, *On Time and Being*, Eng. trans. Joan Stambaugh (New York: Harper & Row, 1972), 55–56.

21. See especially Heidegger, "Letter on Humanism," 294.

22. Heidegger, *Being and Time*, 243.

23. *The Journal of Religious Ethics*, 4/1 (Spring, 1976): 105–30.

24. Thomas W. Ogletree, *The Use of the Bible in Christian Ethics* (Philadelphia: Fortress Press, 1983), 15–46.

25. Chap. 4 in this volume, "The Activity of Interpreting in Moral Judgment," has direct bearing on this problem.

26. Hans Georg-Gadamer, *Truth and Method*, Eng. trans. by Garrett Barden and John Cumming (New York: Seabury Press, 1975), 325–26. The account of interpreting here being set forth depends throughout on Gadamer's accomplishment. See also chap. 1 of *The Use of the Bible in Christian Ethics*, 1–6.

27. In addition to works of Jürgen Habermas cited earlier, special note

might be taken of Alvin W. Gouldner, *The Coming Crisis of Western Sociology* (New York: Basic Books, 1970); Peter Bachrach and Morton Baratz, *Power and Poverty: Theory and Practice* (New York: Oxford University Press, 1970); and Steven Lukes, *Power: A Radical View* (London: MacMillan, 1974).

2

HOSPITALITY TO THE STRANGER: THE ROLE OF THE "OTHER" IN MORAL EXPERIENCE

Both in a theoretical and a practical sense the "other," the personal other, presents the central theme for ethical understanding. Apart from the "other" and the claims which she or he can make upon me, "morality"—if one can call it that—is but the shrewd management of life's exigencies in light of my more or less arbitrary personal preferences. Whether it be refined and subtle and sophisticated, or careless and thoughtless and unreflective, such morality finally boils down to egoism, the assessment and utilization of all aspects of the world in terms of my own purposes. It is the "other" addressing me who alone can shake and call into question my egoism, requiring me to take into account another center of meaning and valuation, another orientation onto the world, in making my own decisions and in carrying out my own actions.

Virtually all ethical perspectives of note in Western thought have sought to take the "other" into account. Rarely, however, is the other's call or appeal taken as the privileged instance which opens up the original meaning of morality itself. Characteristically, even when this phenomenon is given considerable weight, it is assimilated into other frames of reference—a principle of rationality, enlightened self-interest, the dynamics of self-constitution, a general theory of values, "causes" to which the self is loyal. These latter frames of reference are taken to be the decisive ones for uncovering the moral quality of human experience, including its social forms as well. Against this dominant tendency of ethical thought, the aim of this essay is to highlight the originality of the self-other interaction, more particularly the "other's" appeal in that interaction, for constituting the meaning of morality. Rather than enjoying priority over this central dynamic, the various structures normally brought to light in ethical analysis as essential to moral experience receive their true significance only in relation to this appeal and its fundamental conditions.

The account which follows will draw upon phenomenological descriptions of intersubjectivity for clarifying the nature of moral experience. The analysis will not, however, be philosophical in a sense that is wholly abstracted from theological interests. The principal guide for the constructive proposals is a Jewish thinker—Immanuel Levinas—whose philosophic imagination has been stimulated and enriched by motifs drawn from biblical faith: particularly the eschatological horizon of that faith, but also more specific themes such as covenant, concern for the widow, the fatherless, the poor, and hospitality to the stranger. Given the presence of these motifs, the essay could in H. Richard Niebuhr's sense be characterized as an exercise in Jewish and Christian philosophy—an attempt to give philosophic form to possibilities of understanding opened up by the central symbols and sagas of the Judeo-Christian tradition. Yet the criteria for assessing its results remain philosophic, appealing to the phenomenological notion of evidence.[1] Biblical materials have a suggestive significance, a role in quickening the imagination, but a distinctively theological articulation of the central themes will not be in view.

SOCIAL PARADIGMS OF THE MORAL LIFE

A great deal of attention has been given to self-other interactions by sociologists and social psychologists. On the face of it, these accounts might appear to provide us with all we need for a social interpretation of moral experience. Talcott Parsons's influential functionalist theory builds, for example, on a basic paradigm of interaction between two subjects, ego and alter.[2] Ego acts toward or on alter not simply with a view to the promotion of his own interests; in determining his course of action he also takes into account alter's anticipated response to his action. The sociological problem is to clarify the source and nature of the knowledge which permits both ego and alter mutually to anticipate each other's likely responses to particular actions. The solution is that the ego-alter interaction occurs in a context that is limited and regulated by conditioning and controlling factors which ego and alter have more or less in common. The conditioning factors are linked to basic physiological, psychological, and economic needs whose relative gratification is requisite to the effective functioning of both ego and alter. The controlling factors are linked to cultural patterns which specify appropriate courses of action for various types of actors. These patterns embody more general values in defining good and right action among human beings.[3] They include specifically moral values. Moral values then are ingredient in the control factors which provide order and stability to human interactions. Without the operation of these factors, human interaction would be virtually impossible since ego would have no basis for estimating either the meaning a particular action might have for alter or alter's likely response to that action.

The power of these culturally mediated norms for regulating action is further clarified when the emergence of selfhood is itself shown to be integrally connected with the internalization of cultural patterns in a socialization process.[4] Becoming a subject capable of interaction with other subjects involves incorporating into one's own subjectivity typical understandings of appropriate human behavior for various kinds of actors in various kinds of situations. Thus, moral experience comes to have direct reference to cultural norms. These norms constitute a "third" reality which underlies, facilitates, and regulates human interactions. The third reality is the medium within which self-other relationships take place. It limits the egoism of human actors, in a sense "programming" them to take the typical interests and needs of various types of others into account in their actions. To be socialized, to internalize a culture in one's sense of selfhood, is to be able to engage in social interactions in a manner that leaves space for the life quests of both ego and alter.

What is significant about these accounts is that they highlight the inescapable presence of moral factors in ordinary, everyday human interactions. Apart from morality, there can be no selfhood, nor any interactions which are, properly speaking, social. What is insufficient about these accounts is that the operations they bring into view concern only the more or less conventional forms of moral experience, those forms which are already sedimented in a culture and hence, provide order and stability in human relationships. As important as these operations may be to social existence, they do not in themselves display the possibilities of criticism and innovation in moral experience. Insofar as established patterns protect human actors from violation at the hands of others, and provide channels within which actions to enhance life can be pursued, they merit endorsement in critical ethical reflection. Insofar as they violate human actors or render them vulnerable to violations by others, or insofar as they thwart the life quests of human actors, they are subject to challenge in critical ethical reflection. The task is to uncover the possibilities for such criticism; it is to identify the locus of origination in moral experience.[5] How is this locus to be discovered and isolated?

The Parsonsian paradigm was devised to establish some reference points for the construction of a general theory of action which could in turn order work in the human sciences. One would not, therefore, expect an ethical interest to be paramount in its formulation. Nonetheless, this paradigm can provide a map for locating the points in human social experience at which criticism in moral thinking might emerge. Such criticism would in any case arise in the interaction situation. The crucial reference point for its appearance might, therefore, be "ego" or the action of ego, "alter" or the response of alter, the conditioning and controlling factors which limit and regulate the interactions between ego and alter, or a combination of some or all of these loci.

In seeking to identify the possibilities of criticism, there are strong grounds for granting primacy to the conditioning and controlling factors noted in the paradigm. These factors will necessarily figure in criticism since they provide essential resources for such criticism. Moreover, criticism is not likely to emerge in a society, at least not in an effective form, unless there are contradictions or at least strains within or between these two sets of factors. Criticism has a stronger possibility of appearing if the basic conditions for life in a society are "out of phase" with the dominant value orientations of the culture. In a situation of this kind, conventional moral norms are apt to prescribe and also justify behavior which is alienating or oppressive to at least some actors in a society. The experience of alienation will then provide an impulse to criticism and innovation.[6] Likewise, strains or contradictions within the established value patterns of a culture may themselves provide occasions for criticism leading to innovative moral thought. Of special importance in this regard are contradictions which set the more concrete rituals and rules of everyday interactions—the manners of a society—in opposition to the general value orientations which legitimate those rituals and rules.[7]

Specialists in ethics have rightly given a good deal of energy to analyzing both basic life conditions in human society and value patterns in human culture as a means of uncovering resources for ethical criticism. In many cases attempts have also been made to establish trans-cultural understandings of values which might have relevance for sorting out unsolved value conflicts within a given culture. Even so, the conditioning and controlling factors in the interaction paradigm cannot in themselves function as sources of origination in moral experience even though they are quite essential as resources for such origination. Neither ideas nor basic life conditions have as such the power of origination. This power presupposes subjects, centered selves. Thus, Alfred Schutz correctly notes that the typifications governing human interactions can be questioned and modified only in the "we relation," in face-to-face encounters in which ego and alter are reciprocally attentive to each other.[8] The task is to determine more precisely how the possibilities for origination in moral experience become actualized in this encounter.

MORALITY AS SELF-CONSTITUTION

The dominant tendency in Western ethics has been to accent the self-constitution of ego, the moral actor, in establishing the possibilities for criticism and innovation in moral experience. The "other" takes on significance largely because of the essential role he or she plays in this process. The moral interests of the other are not overlooked. Yet they derive their force primarily from the moral actor's own identification with the other and his projection of his own sense of moral worth on that other.

Paul Tillich's thought can represent this line of thinking. His work contains all of the reference points in Parsons' paradigm of social interaction, though now developed in terms of an ontology. The key categories are individuation and participation, understood as elements in the basic self-world structure of being. Being-itself undergirds, embraces, and transcends this fundamental polarity. Being-itself is interpreted, moreover, in terms of both power and meaning, the former suggesting the conditioning factors which enable human interactions, the latter indicating the controlling factors which regulate these interactions. Even so, in unfolding his understanding of moral experience Tillich draws upon this structure chiefly to uncover the dynamics involved in the self-constitution of the moral agent. It is largely in relation to these dynamics that the other enters into his account of moral experience.

Morality, Tillich suggests, is "the function of life in which the centered self constitutes itself as a person." It is "the totality of those acts in which a potentially personal life process becomes an actual person."[9] How and under what circumstances does the centered self constitute itself as a person? In the encounter with an other, Tillich answers, the other "who is already and not yet a person." "Personal life," he continues, "emerges in the encounter of person with person and in no other way."[10] My encounter with the other person is not only the essential occasion for my achievement of personhood—a point already well established within social psychology; it also implies an unconditional *command* to acknowledge the other whom I encounter as a person like me, as a center of meaning and valuation toward the world having its own dignity and integrity. The argument seems to be that I can achieve centeredness as a person only in interaction with others who are also in the process of becoming persons. An essential condition for the realization and maintenance of my being as a person is that I enter into relationships with other persons. Yet I can be in relation with other persons only if I in turn respect them in their personhood. Thus, the dynamics of my own personhood bind me to an unconditional obligation to act with full regard for the personhood of the other selves whom I encounter.

Tillich completes his basic description by distinguishing between encounters which are only potentially personal and those which are actually personal and as such capable both of constituting the self as a moral self and also of disclosing the unconditional validity of the moral imperative. Personal encounters, he contends, involve a participation in the other one. The reference to participation reflects Tillich's attempt to move beyond a purely formal understanding of the moral imperative as the obligation to recognize in the other an inviolable limit to the self's appropriation of the world through its own centering processes. The material meaning of the moral imperative emerges through the self's participation in the lives of other selves. The morally significant participation, moreover, does not stem from a merely chance discovery of personal characteristics shared in common. It is the self's participation in the *center* of the other self, and consequently, an acceptance of that self in his or her particularities regardless of whether a convergence of personal characteristics is present. Such acceptance, Tillich suggests, is the core meaning of agape love. It indicates the essential meaning of the moral imperative *and* the decisive condition for the actualization of personhood.[11]

There are many appealing features in Tillich's analysis. Yet it contains subtle movements which are troublesome and, I believe, finally quite unsatisfactory. To begin with, Tillich initiates his discussion by speaking of encounters in which the self *experiences* the validity of the moral imperative. He ends by calling attention to agape relationships, not to characterize encounters *actually experienced*, but to indicate a moral imperative. This imperative expresses an essential possibility of selfhood which *ought* to be determinative for our lives even though under the conditions of existence it does not find actualization, except perhaps fragmentarily. Consequently, we still do not find in Tillich's work an account of the actual manifestation of the material meaning of the moral imperative in the concrete encounter between persons. What is even more disappointing is that Tillich, while seeming to give central place to the I-thou encounter in the constitution of moral experience, continually subordinates that encounter to the dynamics of self-integration. In the final analysis the latter dynamics, not the I-thou encounter, provide the key to the meaning of moral experience. Despite the talk about participating in the center of the other or of accepting the other, it is not clear, in other words, that the other has moral significance for the self except insofar as he or she is a function of that self's own thrust toward self-actualization. What is missing in this presentation is a fuller appreciation of the *de-centering* of perspective which is involved in the I-thou encounter, especially if that encounter embraces what Tillich characterizes as a participation in the other's center of being.

It would be inappropriate to belittle the importance of self-integration for the moral life. To be a moral agent at all one must in significant measure be a centered self. Apart from such centering, we would have little or no capacity to act at all. We would rather be governed in our behavior by some combination of our impulses and the various sanctions applied to us by those around us. The precondition for the free act, which is entailed by morality, is relative success in achieving the self-integration of life. Nonetheless, this centering of selfhood, even though it depends upon positive interactions with significant others over a period of time, is not in itself the key to the meaning of moral experience. It rather specifies an essential condition for the possibility of such experience. Moral experience in itself, precisely because it stems from openness to the other's center, consists in our transcendence of our own centers of being, and thus, in a suspension of the self-integrative processes which make it up. It involves a recognition in the other of a center of meaning and value which cannot legitimately be reduced in significance to our own drives for self-actualization. What is needed is an account of moral experience which permits us to see the originality of the other's claim upon the self, the other's capacity to decenter the self in its own orientation to the world, to present the self with value meanings which it cannot assimilate into its own processes of world constitution. Tillich's ontology suggests the importance of this line of investigation, though Tillich has not himself accomplished what is required.

Interestingly enough, Jean-Paul Sartre—who attaches no special moral weight to participation in the other's center of being—manages to capture more effectively than Tillich the decentering of perspective which is central to the moral relation with another self. In Sartre's account the encounter with the other produces a sense of shock, a disorientation with respect to the world. The instance Sartre uses to surface this phenomenon is well known. A man is looking through a keyhole. He is totally absorbed in the scene he is viewing. So complete is his orientation to that scene that he has lost all self-consciousness about what he is doing. Suddenly he hears a footstep. Someone else is coming. He will now be caught in the act of spying. He feels shame. The shame is not an indication that he considers himself to be guilty of some wrong-doing. The deeper problem, Sartre suggests, is that a self who has the power to constitute the meaning of his world finds that the meaning of his own act is being constituted by another center of consciousness. The other will define, interpret, assess, and evaluate his action. He will become an object to that consciousness and so lose control over the meaning of his own being.[12] The encounter between persons, Sartre is claiming, far from bearing the euphoric promise of self-actualization in community, discloses a situation of tragic conflict. The conflict may be latent or only threatened, but it is the underlying structural reality in any meeting between two centers of freedom. Either I define for myself the meaning of my world, and in good faith take responsibility for my attitudes toward the world and my actions in it—in which case I also determine the meaning of the humanity of all others; or I let others determine the meaning of my being and my actions, and in bad faith flee the responsibility inherent in my freedom. The other is thus essentially a threat to my own centeredness in my world, a decentralization of the world, Sartre says, that undermines the centralization which I am simultaneously effecting.[13]

For Sartre as well as for Tillich morality is linked to the self-integration of life. The critical contrast which he highlights is between good faith and bad faith: accepting or denying the radical implications of my freedom, constituting the meaning of my world or letting that meaning be determined by others.[14] Unlike Tillich, however, Sartre finds no fundamental harmony between the self-integration of life and the I-thou encounter. Participating in the other's center, if not an ontological impossibility, is at least bad faith, an act of giving myself over to the meaning-constituting activity of the other. Not surprisingly, Sartre sees no possibility for the agape love which Tillich identifies as the central content of the moral imperative. Love, he contends, is essentially narcissistic. It is my attempt to seduce the other into loving me, into affirming and valuing me in my own centeredness. It is my effort to lure the other into bad faith, perhaps as a defense against that other's threat to my own freedom.

Nothing in Sartre's account, it should be emphasized, precludes an appreciation of the social-psychological insight that selves emerge in interaction with other selves. For Sartre as well as for Tillich self-consciousness, and hence also freedom, is made possible through the encounter with other centers of consciousness. What Sartre refuses to conclude from this fact—and what Tillich perhaps concludes too easily—is that persons are most fully actualized in a community with other persons, a community manifesting agape love. In Sartre's account, the more persons are centered in their beings, the greater the likelihood that the latent conflict between them as centers of freedom will become manifest; the less persons are so centered, on the other hand, the more likely it is that one or both will exist in bad faith under the legitimating cover of conventional morality. Sartre, we could say, has provided an analysis of human existence at the level of ontology which in all essential respects confirms the earlier portrait of Thomas Hobbes: the state of nature is a state of war![15]

For Protestant theological perspectives, it might be noted, the dissolution of a structural basis in human experience for the self-giving love called forth by the gospel is neither particularly surprising nor especially disturbing. Within this perspective neighbor love in the pattern of Christ's love is simply not a human possibility. Should this kind of love appear among human beings at all, it can only be viewed as a strange and alien possibility of grace, a fruit of the presence of Jesus Christ. It is only through Christ, Dietrich Bonhoeffer has argued, that I can approach my neighbor.[16] Christ has secured my existence by grace through faith. He has thus freed me to approach my neighbor in openness without any need to exploit or dehumanize, and also without any possibility of being exploited or dehumanized myself, at least not in the ultimate sense. In this frame of reference it is Christ who decenters me from my egoistic orientation to life, and in the process makes room in my life for my fellow human beings. Apart from the grace of God, the prudent are surely those who acknowledge the brokenness of the world and take self-interest to be the base point of all human action.

There are important respects in which I take these Christian affirmations to be true. They express the ambiguity of the human condition and indicate a theological basis for the hope that the destructive features of human life might be overcome. I would, however, find unsatisfactory any suggestion that Christian forms of love and caring are in no way possible as modes of being in the fundamental structures and processes which make up human moral experience. In this respect, I share Tillich's insistence that the moral law be interpreted as expressing the claims of essential

being over against estranged existence, and that human fulfillment be understood as including reconciliation with the essential possibilities of human being. The task remains that of uncovering the constitution of moral experience in self-other
interactions.

MORALITY AS RECEPTIVITY TO THE
APPEAL OF THE "OTHER"

I have been explicating what I take to be a dominant tradition
in Western ethics, the delineation of the meaning of moral experience, especially the possibilities for origination in such experience, with primary reference to the self-constitution of the
moral agent. This account provides a context in which we can
appreciate the importance of Immanuel Levinas's investigations
of self-other relations. Like Sartre, Levinas fully appreciates the
decentering of perspective effected by the presence of the other.
Unlike Sartre, he reads this occurrence not as a threat to personal
integrity, but as a summons to moral existence. Morality begins
precisely when my egoism has been called into question and I
learn to take the other into account. And egoism in this context
refers not to selfishness in a crass sense, but to any process, however refined, in which I remain the decisive and controlling reference point for the meaning and value of the world. Levinas's
more dramatic way of making his point is to assert that morality
begins when I become more concerned about not committing
murder than about avoiding death.[17] In this frame of reference
it is the initiative of the other that opens up to me the possibility
of moral experience. The weight has shifted from ego to alter in
the self-other interaction. How does Levinas develop his understanding?

Levinas's starting point is not the self's quest for centeredness,
nor even the reaching out of the self for response and confirmation by the other. It is the presence of the other taken as a
novel phenomenon. Levinas does not, however, represent the
other in terms of the look, the look which distances, alienates,
and finally objectifies and dehumanizes. He focuses attention on
the *face* of the other, the face taken as the locus of the other's
expression as subject.[18] In Husserlian language, the other's face
appresents his or her subjective orientation onto the world. The
key mode of expression among human beings is discourse, more

particularly, discourse using language. Its aim, Levinas reminds us, is not to objectify, but to communicate, to establish relation.

What is communicated in discourse is not in the first instance the other's selfhood in its interior being. Levinas is far more reluctant than Tillich to speak of my possibility of entering into the center of another being, or even of assuming that the other's center can or should become accessible to me. Such language suggests a suffocating familiarity inappropriate to the infinity which characterizes the human form of being. What comes to expression in discourse is an interpretation of the world and of its meaning and value. Thus, I relate to the other in and through the world, certainly through the meanings we share in common, but more significantly, through the meanings the other is able to open up to me, meanings to which I would otherwise have no access at all. It is the result of the other's meaning-constituting activity that is communicated in discourse.[19]

Oddly enough, Levinas notes, it makes no difference to the understanding of moral experience whether the other is lying, dissembling, or speaking as truly as possible in this communication. What is in any case disclosed to me in the face of the other is his or her subjective orientation onto the world.[20] Moreover, since the communication consists in the discourse of a self-transcending subjectivity, it is not objectifiable, nor is it at my disposal to appropriate and interpret as I see fit. The other must rather continually come to the aid of her own expression, interpreting it, elaborating it, explaining it, placing it more fully in context, indeed, expanding, altering, and possibly repudiating it as an expression which failed or perhaps deceived, whether intentionally or unintentionally. Every communication, in short, entails on-going communication if it is indeed the communication of a free subject.[21]

The import of the other's expression in discourse is that it calls into question my egoism, which includes the sovereignty of my own meaning-constituting activity toward the world. It confronts me with an appeal to take into account another center of meaning in my own understanding of the world, a center which in the nature of the case cannot be assimilated into my own processes of self-integration. In this context Levinas challenges thinkers, such as Sartre, who give sovereign place to freedom as the crux of morality. According to Levinas, Sartre rightly uses the phrase "pour soi," the "for itself," to designate his understanding of the free subject. Sartre's free subject, he suggests is for itself as in the slogan "every man for himself," for itself as in the "famished stomach that has no ears," capable of killing for a crust of bread, for itself as the surfeited one who does not understand the starving and approaches them as an alien species.[22] My freedom, he contends, is not an innocent spontaneity, but a usurper and a murderer, a violent and arbitrary exercise of power. It requires justification before and in the presence of the other. For Sartre, my freedom is absolute; the other's freedom confronts me as a problem, a threat. For Levinas, freedom as such is arbitrary and unjustified until it has been subjected to the claims of the other. Justice is thus prior to freedom in moral experience.[23]

How shall I respond to the other's appeal which questions my freedom? Obviously, I can and often do resist the other's resistance to me. Perhaps I aggressively reassert my own sovereignty over against the alien claim of the other; perhaps I filter out the otherness of that claim and assimilate the other once more to my own project, my own frame of reference. I can seek to annul the plurality of the world. Yet the commencement of moral consciousness is manifest in another response, a readiness to welcome the other, to show hospitality to the stranger. Such openness to the other carries its own form of shock, "a traumatism of astonishment," Levinas calls it.[24] But the shock does not reflect my sudden discomfort at the other's unexpected challenge to my sovereign freedom. It reflects my painful discovery of the murderous implications of my own egoistic self-absorption. Conscience emerges in response to the other's moral resistance to my arbitrary freedom. For Levinas as well as for Sartre shame manifests the self's awareness of the impact of the other's presence. Yet in his view shame does not disclose a sense of merely being exposed to the other's definitions and evaluations. It discloses my remorse over my insensitivity to the meaning of the other's expression. I discover that I have valued freedom more than justice, enjoyment more than goodness. The point is that the commencement of moral consciousness—and, I think we could add, its continual recommencement—always takes place in contexts in which my egoism has reigned supreme. If conscience as a sense of justice and regard for the other is to emerge, it must do so through the overcoming of the self-interestedness of the "for itself." The moral encounter, far from being the occasion for my self-integration, involves, therefore, an unsettling decentering of my being, opening me to plurality, indeed, to infinity in the self-transcending presence of the other.

One of Levinas's most creative contributions is to call attention to the asymmetry of the interpersonal relations that mark the commencement of moral consciousness. The person I meet in a moral mode is both higher and lower than I am: higher in the sense that she summons me to conscience and judges the arbitrariness of my freedom; lower in the sense that she approaches me not with the power to coerce, but in destitution and with supplication, offering no resistance other than a moral one.[25] This suggestion needs explication. The moreness of the other is represented by Levinas in a number of images: the other approaches me in a dimension of height. He is my master, my teacher. More dramatically still, to engage in discourse with an other is to speak with a god! What is Levinas getting at? His point seems to be that the moral encounter with the other opens up a new world of meaning to which I otherwise have no access. I do not possess that world within my own orientation to meaning, not even latently. Thus, I cannot presume that the other is like me or that I can understand the other on the analogy of my own experience—perhaps through a process of identification and projection. If I am to approach the other's world of meaning, I must let him teach me about it, open its contours and nuances to me. Indeed, given the other's power of self-transcendence, he must permanently have the status of my master and teacher if I am to follow the continuously upholding horizons of meaning which make up the world he is constituting.

Levinas is in effect generalizing to all personal encounters the point Søren Kierkegaard made about the decisiveness of the moment for learning the truth. If the moment is not decisive, Kierkegaard argued, it is because in principle we are already in the truth. Our teachers, like Socrates, are merely midwives to facilitate our gaining possession of what in fact is already ours. Inquiry into the truth is essentially *anamnesis*, remembering what has been forgotten. But if the moment is decisive, then apart from the moment we have no relation to the truth, nor do we possess the means for gaining such a relation. We may even be in a polemical posture toward the truth. To gain the truth, we require a teacher who mediates to us that which we could not otherwise have. Indeed, in the latter case, being in the truth means being in relation with the teacher who is the bearer of the truth. For Kierkegaard, of course, the bearer of the truth is Jesus Christ.[26]

In like manner, Levinas is suggesting that we cannot gain access to the being of the other or the world of meaning and value constituted by that other through a process of self-discovery. Here too the encounter, better, the relation, is decisive. Not even the uncovering of my rational essence gives me access to the other, unless I mistakenly assume with Immanuel Kant that the operation of reason is everywhere the same, or that the actualization by all persons of their rational potential would automatically issue in a kingdom of ends.[27] If I would not reduce the other to likeness with me and presume that all persons are essentially the same, then I can learn of the other only by permitting that other to be my master and teacher. Levinas is giving us an account of humanness which embraces plurality. To read and interpret others solely in terms of our own worlds of meaning and value is to do them violence, to objectify them, to reduce them to sameness with everything else. Ethnocentricity is egoism in a cultural mode.

Levinas is not ruling out the possibility of shared meanings, not even the notion of objective knowledge of an objective world. He is calling attention to the fact that discourse, intersubjective communication, founds objectivity and is the sole medium through which shared meanings are able to emerge. These shared meanings can and do include value orientations which have been institutionalized in society. In a sense we could speak of the typifications which regulate human interactions in a society as sedimentations of the results of discourse in face-to-face relationships. It is from their origin in discourse that these typifications derive their moral authority. Even so, as sedimentations of intersubjective expressions, they are, like all discourse, ever subject to interpretation, correction, modification, even radical repudiation, in the ongoing processes of social communication between free subjects.

In the same vein, it is also important to recognize that Levinas is not calling into question the importance of rationality in human interactions. He is simply challenging understandings of rationality which reduce otherness to sameness. Rationality takes on its proper significance when it is placed in the context of discourse. Here it concerns stability and fidelity in relationships. It is not a vehicle of understanding by means of which I can master the logic of the possibilities of human being and so determine what is legitimate or illegitimate about the other's world of meaning. To learn of that world of meaning I must learn from the other, and I must learn on the basis of his expressions. I cannot merely project my own perceptions and understandings upon that other. The readiness to learn from the other, to be a disciple, is thus a crucial moment in the ethical relation to the other. It is the moment by means of which the moral imperative gains its material content. Levinas sums up his analysis by saying that justice is prior to truth, or better, justice is the essential precondition for gaining the truth.[28]

In the commencement of moral experience the other is not only higher than I. He is also in important respects lower, the destitute one who entreats me to have regard for his condition. In this dimension the prototype for the other is the widow, the orphan, the poor, the stranger in the gate, or to embrace Matthew's account of the parable of the judgment, also the hungry, the thirsty, the naked, the sick, the prisoner. In this modality the other is manifest as one who is in no position to bargain or negotiate a fair exchange, as one who has no power to coerce me to give him his due. He is wholly dependent upon my goodness for his well-being. In our actual interactions with persons we rarely, of course, encounter one so destitute. Even the poor of the earth always have the potential for avenging the wrong done to them, which may explain why the privileged view them with hostility and hold them in contempt. Yet the other who can bargain with me or threaten me cannot call my egoism into question, nor can she awaken in me a moral consciousness. She can only remind me of the importance of prudence in pursuing my self-interest. In contrast, the destitute one, provided I am open with him, reveals to me the secret of my egoism and summons me to judgment. He reminds me, for example, of how little I am prepared to do for strictly moral reasons. This experience of judgment gives rise to responsibility. Levinas says infinite responsibility. My responsibility is infinite in the sense that it increases in the measure that I assume it. Likewise, my duties become greater in the degree to which I accomplish them.[29] In Levinas's account it is not clear that there are any limits to this extension of responsibility to and for the other. The "I" arises in enjoyment. It is a separated being having in itself the center around which its existence gravitates. It is confirmed in its singularity, however, by purging itself of this gravitation. In purging itself interminably of its self-absorption, Levinas concludes, the self becomes goodness.[30]

Levinas makes no reference in his description of moral experience to my need for the other—for example, to confirm my personhood. The motive for doing justice to the other and for loving the other does not arise from the fact that the other is an essential factor in my own achievement of self-integration. There are, to be sure, significant others—especially in the family—who have played and continue to play a role in my own self-constitution. But insofar as my relations with others are governed by my need for them, my relation to them is not yet moral. The genuinely moral relation expresses a surplus of being beyond the categories of need. Levinas uses the term "desire" to express this surplus, not a happy choice from my standpoint. He seems to have in mind a dynamic similar to the Platonic "eros" or the Augustinian "caritas." The desire for the other emerges out of my original recognition of the other's value.

MORALITY AND EGOISM

How is Levinas's radical notion of the self's responsibility to the other to be related to egoism, to the moral actor's own quest for self-actualization? Does the moral agent have no rights of her own, no claims that she can legitimately make against the other? The question is an urgent one since in shifting the locus of origination in moral experience from the dynamics of self-integration to the call of the other, the moral subject appears to lose all rights before the other. If the former position tends to turn the other into a function of an essentially egoistic quest for self-actualization, the latter appears to involve an unwarranted surrender of the self and its values to the interests of the other.

Levinas's treatment of the relation of egoism to morality is sketchy and in my judgment finally unsatisfactory; yet several elements in his thinking can be noted. First, a developed egoism, an egoism of enjoyment, seems for Levinas to be an essential precondition for moral experience. If morality cannot be identified with the process of becoming a person in Tillich's sense, it at least seems to presuppose the achievement of a certain level of centeredness in the self. I can question my egoism and respond morally to the other only after I have in some measure already gained my world in enjoyment. So if egoism is questioned and judged in moral experience, it is also presupposed in such experience. The first word may be: enable enjoyment, and not: be responsible to and for your neighbor. Grace is prior to commandment.

Second, Levinas suggests that the full confirmation of our individuality emerges only in a radical transcendence of all concern for self, including a concern for rights. In this frame of reference egoism is not so much overcome by growth in moral consciousness as it is transformed into an integrity suffused with the power to be radically at the disposal of the other. Yet even this sense of integrity must presuppose and embrace a form of egoistic enjoyment, for in Levinas's terms egoistic enjoyment is the basis of the separateness of the self which is presupposed in moral experience. The transcendence of self-concern, therefore, does not so much mark the end of the possibility of egoistic enjoyment as the termination of the urgent attachment to such enjoyment. For the sake of the other I have the power to give up my enjoyment, and to give it up without resentment or self-hatred.

It is not clear how this image of radical self-giving might be uncovered phenomenologically. It does, however, resonate with portrayals of mature humanness generated by the eschatological horizon of biblical faith. Representative is the self-denial which characterizes discipleship: "He who seeks to save his life will lose it, but he who loses his life for my sake and the gospel's shall find it." But if this possibility is genuinely eschatological, then it must be interpreted with full appreciation for the fact that the eschatological horizon is *not yet* as well as *already*. To demand self-sacrifice from those who are not yet capable of it is not to further moral maturity but to use moral appeals to violate and assault persons. Should such a demand win compliance, the compliance would more likely express self-hatred and resentment than love and justice.[31] Even so, the eschatological summons to the full measure of our humanity remains the disquieting possibility opened up in moral experience. It reminds us that self-realization is self-giving out of fullness, not self-possession; and that its accomplishment is a gift of grace, not a personal achievement.

Third, Levinas has a brief discussion of apology as a feature in my response to the other's judgment on my egoism. Apology has the sense of defense which belongs to the Latin root. It is my attempt to legitimate my egoism over against the other's claim. It is a notion which might suggest that I too have rights which balance the rights of the other. Levinas does not draw this conclusion, however. In the moral relation I cannot establish some third standpoint in terms of which I might assess the moral worth of my own claims in comparison with those of the other. To be sure, society with its laws and rules offers such a standpoint. The notion of equality emerges, Levinas suggests, when a third party attends to my discourse with the other.[32] The third party must balance claims if she or he is to relate to the participants in the original discourse. Yet for moral experience itself, understood in terms of its original appearance, there is no possibility of such balancing. I cannot say, for example, that I have a right to the maximum amount of freedom consistent with a like freedom for all others. Such mutuality is still prudence and not yet morality. It has not yet broken with the egoistic orientation to life. In contrast, Levinas insists, the more I do my duty the fewer rights I have. The notion of apology then does not alter the fundamental asymmetry of the moral relation. It merely reflects my struggle with the awakening of conscience effected by the other. If my apology does legitimate my egoism, it can apparently do so only on the grounds of a necessity I have to fight for the gratification of my own needs as a condition of the possibility for my genuinely moral response to the other.[33]

If I am correctly interpreting Levinas here, I am quite dissatisfied with the outcome of his reflections. While thinkers such as Tillich and Sartre may have a tendency to assimilate the moral significance of the other to the self's own integrative processes, so Levinas seems to have fallen into the opposite error of denying the self any moral right whatever before the other. Egoism, if it has any justification at all, is apparently justifiable solely for the sake of the other and in terms of the other. But if this conclusion is consistently drawn, it is also no longer clear how the other as a subject is himself in a position to make moral claims. Unless a moral right inheres in the other's being as subject, even as a subject of enjoyment, then that other would seem to have no basis for making a claim on me. He could not properly be identified as being a center of value. Yet if value attaches to the other by virtue of his subjectivity, then subjectivity would seem to have the same significance for all moral actors. In short, moral worth must in some fashion attach to subjectivity, even on the terms of Levinas' own account of moral experience. This result brings us back to Tillich's fundamental insight: that morality comes to expression in the self-integration of life, in the realization of personhood.

How shall we relate the contributions of Tillich and Levinas? Tillich calls attention to the fact that value of a distinctive sort attaches to personhood. The centered self is a distinctive locus of value by virtue of the fact that she is in herself a center of valuation toward the world. Better, the centered self is a meaning- and value-constituting subjectivity; which is to say, the appearance of values presupposes subjective acts of valuation. Since valuative acts are always given with value meanings, then subjects capable of such acts have a unique status in the realm of values. They do not simply make up one set of values within the multiplicity and heterogeneity of value types. As centers of consciousness, they provide an essential condition for the possibility of the appearance of any values whatever.

Levinas's account of moral experience requires a prior apprehension of the distinctive value of persons in some such fashion as this, not only for the "other" who makes his appeal, but also for the self to whom the appeal is addressed. Levinas provides the materials for an understanding of this kind in his discussion of enjoyment. In his thought, enjoyment, indeed, egoistic enjoyment, is the phenomenal ground for the separateness of the self which is presupposed in intersubjective encounters. Yet he obscures the senses in which worth of a distinctively moral sort attaches to enjoyment. He writes as though egoistic enjoyment has no rights in face of the claims of the other, that in becoming goodness the self totally surrenders its own rights, extending itself without limit in responsibility to the other. The problem is to clarify how the self as a center of egoistic enjoyment might also take on moral worth, even to the point of placing *moral* limits on the claims of the other.

I have suggested that the centered self is a distinctive locus of value by virtue of its meaning-constituting activity. Yet the value which attaches to the self in this activity is not in itself properly to be called *moral* value, at least not without further qualification. I would not, therefore, follow Tillich in identifying morality with the self-integration of life. Peculiarly moral values emerge in the decentering of perspective which is effected by the call of the other. Here one center of valuation confronts another. Morality concerns the clarification of the normative implications of this confrontation. The criticism of Levinas is not, therefore, that he links the commencement of morality to this encounter. It is that he seems to resolve the moral issues raised in the encounter wholly in favor of the other. Yet insofar as the moral subject in this encounter (ego) is also a center of valuation of intrinsic worth, it is not apparent that the resolution of conflict between the self and the other must necessarily move in the direction indicated by Levinas.

This point can be clarified by returning to Levinas's notion of apology—the self's attempt to justify itself before the other who has called it into question. I would suggest that the apology need not be a feeble one, that it can take on moral force of its own as a response to the other's appeal. Nor need the apology be limited in its legitimacy to the self's plea for the opportunity to pursue its own development to the degree that is requisite for a moral orientation to the other. The one who apologizes for his egoism is in himself a center of meaning and value, indeed, a self-transcending subject who continually constitutes meaning and value, and then in transcending freedom absolves himself from those meanings, only to return once more to aid them with new interpretations and qualifications. What is at stake here is a dialogic process in which the self as a result of the other's appeal is enabled to clarify his own rights in relation to those of that other. I am a center of freedom, but my freedom must be justified and it must be justified before the other. That is to say, I can only begin to understand the nature and the extent of my own rights by examining them, testing them, and criticizing them in light of the orientation of others—most especially the strangers and aliens, or in general, those who are most likely to be victimized by my egoistic enjoyments. Such others help me to sort out the violent or potentially violent features of my egoism from those which are pacific. The claim is not that I must let others determine who I am and what values and commitments are appropriate for my life. I must finally take responsibility for myself in these matters. Yet it is only in relation to the other, in and through the novelty of the other's orientation to the world, that I can responsibly determine what goodness is for me. Thus, even my egoism gains a qualified justification, justification as my right to the enjoyment of my world and its good. But the justification comes only from and through the other.[34]

This modification in Levinas's thought is, I believe, compatible with his central discovery: that the locus of origination in moral experience is the call of the other. Yet it unfolds that insight in a way that permits a determination of moral limits to the claims which an other can legitimately make against a moral actor. Apart from this modification, the oppressed could not on Levinas's terms legitimately assert their rights against their oppressors, especially when such oppressors believed (as is commonly the case) either that they deserved their special advantages, or that the social inequities in which they participated were somehow necessary to the good of the whole. Nor could a notion of moral community be articulated, community in which the asymmetry of the moral relation is continually reciprocated in mutual respect and care by persons bound together in covenant.

The possibility that the other's appeal will extend my responsibility to that radical limit of self-sacrifice is still not abrogated. With regard to the infinite enlargement of responsibility, Levinas is likely to be irresistible for those nurtured in biblical faith. Should a sacrifice of this kind become morally necessary and also morally possible, it need not in principle be incompatible with egoistic enjoyment, though in actual practice it will almost certainly appear to be so. The self's freedom always embraces the possibility that moral sacrifice, rather than negating egoistic enjoyment, will transfigure and ennoble it—that life will be discovered and embraced in the power to give it up for the sake of the other.

There is one other link between Tillich and Levinas which deserves mention. As we have seen, Tillich roots the imperative to love the other in the fact that relation with the other is an essential component in the self-integration of life. Thus, it is in part my need for the other, and precisely as other, which motivates me to honor norms of love and justice in my dealings with that other. In contrast, Levinas argues that the moral relation with the other involves a surplus, a form of desire which radically transcends need. Insofar as I am related to the other in terms of my need for him, he is suggesting, I will invariably seek to draw that other narcissistically into my own orientation to meaning and value. If I am to be open to the other, to show hospitality to the stranger, then I must be moved by a desire which surpasses need.

Levinas's point is important in what it affirms. Yet once again he has overstated his case. For if the moral relation with the other is pure surplus, then it also tends to become purely contingent, to lack any fundamental necessity in human relations. The surplus soon becomes superfluous. The problem is that Levinas portrays as a dichotomy what is in fact a dialectic. On the one hand, need grounds desire, giving it both its fundamental impulse and also its necessity in human life processes. On the other hand, desire transcends need, yet without wholly losing its rootage in the dynamics of need. Indeed, in its transcendence of need, it actually contributes to the realization of the relation which is the proper object of the need in the first place. We can go even further in this vein. If, as Levinas suggests, radical self-giving is a form of self-confirmation, then we apparently have a complex kind of need to give to the other in order to express fully the kind of beings we are. The surplus satisfies a unique kind of lack. Desire fulfills a need.[35] In short, in describing the structure of moral experience, Tillich and Levinas tend to accent opposing poles in a fundamental dialectic. Yet capturing the movement in the dialectic may provide a truer description of moral experience. That movement directs us neither to self-integration nor to openness to the other, but to the dynamics of moral community.

CONCLUSION

I have been seeking in this chapter to identify the locus of origination in moral experience. The primary interest has been to challenge a dominant tendency in Western thinking, linking the possibilities for such origination to the dynamics involved in the self-integration of life. Interpreting morality with reference to the centeredness of the self, I suggested, even when considerable attention is given to interpersonal encounters or to the sociality of the self, inclines us to assimilate the other to the self's own life project. In the process we obscure the decentering of perspective effected by the call or appeal of the other. In contrast, I have highlighted Immanuel Levinas's attempt to locate the commencement of moral consciousness in a readiness to welcome the other, to show hospitality to the stranger. In this frame of reference, morality begins when egoism is judged and called into question, when a self opens itself to the world of meaning communicated by the other and responds in appropriate ways to the other's need quite beyond considerations of personal benefit or danger. This latter perspective, I noted, does not simply set aside an egoistic concern for enjoyment and personal fulfillment. At one level morality presupposes egoism, since egoism enables us to gain the separateness which is the precondition of our power to orient ourselves to others. At a more profound level, egoism is transformed into a confirmation of selfhood which, paradoxically, is effected precisely in the radical capacity for self-giving to the other without limit. Alongside this basic condition and this ultimate possibility, egoism itself gains its right in discourse with the other, a discourse which permits us to sort out the enjoyments which are compatible with moral goodness from those which violate and destroy it.

In developing this alternative account, I have been critical of some of Tillich's work. I do not believe, however, that these ideas are at odds with what Tillich himself accomplished. On the contrary, they can readily be assimilated into the ontological structure which orders Tillich's thought as a whole. With the aid of Levinas's investigations into the moral import of intersubjectivity, I have, I believe, been able to make a substantive contribution to Tillich's own ontology.

In the long run, Levinas's primary achievement may be his singular success in uncovering the moral significance of pluralism at an elemental level of human experience. In challenging radically all lines of thinking which tempt us to assimilate others to our own frames of reference, to interpret them from our own points of view, he offers a profound corrective to the cultural imperialism which is embodied in the ethnocentric character of so much of our thinking. He teaches us to listen, to learn from the other, before determining the moral content of our actions toward those whose worlds of meaning are different than our own.

Accenting the appeal of the other and the moral response to that other as points of origination in moral experience does not, of course, undercut the need for mediation in human interaction. The conditioning and controlling factors in human relationships, which are so important in the social sciences, do indeed belong to the structure of moral experience. Even in the moral relation my approach to the other is always limited and guided by the typifications embodied in the culture that I have internalized in the course of my emergence as a self. These typifications, moreover, will invariably figure materially in any criticisms or transformations of received moral understandings which may arise out of living discourse. Likewise, if the discourse in question impacts profoundly on our ordered patterns of living, it will itself become thematized in a common culture and institutionalized in the typical forms of interaction which order life in human society. Even so, the other's appeal provides the privileged instance for uncovering what is constitutive of moral experience. Grasping what is distinctive about this appeal can, therefore, provide a framework of understanding which will enable us to maintain a moral perspective in approaching the various materials and methods of inquiry that are relevant for developing an ethical theory.

NOTES

1. Cf. Edmund Husserl, *Cartesian Meditations: An Introduction to Phenomenology*, Eng. trans. Dorion Cairns (The Hague: Martinus Nijhoff, 1960), 13–14, 28.
2. Talcott Parsons and Edward Shils, eds., *Toward a General Theory of Action* (New York: Harper & Row, 1962), 105–06. The distinction between conditioning and controlling factors appears in later essays. Cf. "The Concept of Society: The Components and Their Interrelation," in *Politics and Social Structure* (New York: The Free Press, 1969), 32.
3. Cf. Talcott Parsons, "The Place of Ultimate Values in Sociological Theory," *International Journal of Ethics* (1935).
4. The most influential model in American social thought is the one provided by G. H. Mead. Cf. *Mind, Self, and Society* (Chicago: University of Chicago Press, 1934). The impact of Mead's thought on persons such as H. Richard Niebuhr and Gibson Winter is well known. A similar perspective in a phenomenological context is provided by Maur-

ice Merleau-Ponty in "The Child's Relations with Others," in *The Primacy of Perception*, ed. James M. Edie (Evanston, Ill.: Northwestern University Press, 1964), 96–158.

5. As I see it, H. Richard Niebuhr (*The Responsible Self: An Essay in Christian Moral Philosophy* [New York: Harper & Row, 1963]) largely adopts a social science model for describing moral experience. He differs from a thinker such as Parsons in that he highlights the possibilities for critical moral judgment which are present in the conditioning and controlling factors underlying human interactions. Of particular importance is his interpretation of radical monotheism as the decisive referent for the "third" which governs human interactions. In this respect, Niebuhr's *Radical Monotheism and Western Culture* (New York: Harper and Brothers, 1960), should be read with *The Responsible Self*.

6. See Chalmers Johnson, *Revolutionary Change* (Boston: Little, Brown & Co., 1966), for a Parsonsian account of the implications of this sort of conflict for social change.

7. The classic instance of a full-scale analysis of this sort is Gunner Myrdal's *An American Dilemma* (New York: Harper and Brothers, 1944).

8. Cf., e.g., Schutz and Luckmann, *Structure of the Life-World*, 64–68.

9. Paul Tillich, *Systematic Theology*, vol. 3: *Life and the Spirit, History and the Kingdom of God* (Chicago: University of Chicago Press, 1963), 38.

10. Ibid., 40.

11. Ibid., 45–46.

12. Jean-Paul Sartre, *Being and Nothingness*, Eng. trans. Hazel E. Barnes (New York: Philosophical Library, 1956), 259–73.

13. Ibid., 255.

14. Actually Sartre himself does not treat the distinction between "good faith" and "bad faith" as a moral distinction at all. It is an ontological distinction. It designates two fundamental possibilities given with the peculiarity of the human mode of being, more precisely, with the negating power of consciousness. Thus, Sartre is by no means saying that we ought to set aside "bad faith" and to strive for "good faith." He assumes that our characteristic stance will be "bad faith," and that "good faith" can in no case be sustained as a stable life pattern. As a moral point of view, what Sartre offers is a tragic vision, an account of our inescapable immersion in self-deception and illusion. The most we can hope to attain is occasional insight into this tragic knot, something akin to a cathartic occurrence of self-recognition. For a good account of this tragic vision, see Stephen Crites, "The Aesthetics of Self-Deception," *Soundings* 62/2 (Summer 1979): 107–29, especially 112–19. On this point Sartre is profoundly at odds with the Christian understanding of the essential non-necessity of the human self-immersion in evil.

15. As the last two centuries of social and political thought have made clear, this gloomy conclusion does not undermine the possibility of developing an ethic which clarifies our obligations to others! What it does establish is that the starting point for such an ethic must be some version of enlightened self-interest. Thus, the argument goes, my own integrity and my own well-being will be better served in the long run if I act with respect for other persons and also devote some energy to the promotion of their well-being. In capitalistic and democratic societies, self-interestedness has characteristically been transformed into social responsibility and accountability through some version of the social contract—a contract which self-interested persons would reasonably choose as the best means of pursuing their own goals. Constitution making is, therefore, an important feature in the political life of such societies. John Rawls's *Theory of Justice* (Cambridge: Harvard University Press, 1971) is a most effective recent attempt to develop the logic in this line of thinking. In socialist societies and in socio-political movements inspired by Marxist thought, self-interest is overcome by taking it up into class interest, replacing bourgeois individualism with class solidarity. In his *Critique de la raison dialectique: précédé de question de méthode* (Paris: Gallimard, 1960), Sartre has himself tried to demonstrate the compatibility of a Marxist class analysis with his own radical ontology of freedom. In both strategies, however, the other's moral importance is at least indirectly a function of a particular actor's quest for self-actualization.

Of the two basic approaches, the collectivist thrust of Marxist thought probably embodies more effectively the decentering of perspective which I associate with moral experience. But it does so essentially by making self-interest collective. In the case of neither perspective does the moral imperative reach beyond the actor's own group, whether that group be defined in terms of a social contract or in terms of class membership. Thus, the solution to the disturbing presence of the other is to minimize the decentering of perspective which is effected by that other's presence.

16. Cf., e.g., Dietrich Bonhoeffer, *Life Together*, Eng. trans. John W. Doberstein (New York: Harper and Brothers, 1954), 21–26.

17. Immanuel Levinas, *Totality and Infinity: An Essay on Exteriority*, Eng. trans. Alphonso Lingis (Pittsburgh, Pa.: Duquesne University Press, 1969), 47.

18. Ibid., 66 et al.

19. Ibid., 202. Edmund Husserl's studies of intersubjectivity clarify the phenomenological bases of this claim. Husserl isolates acts of consciousness as points of orientation on the world. It is from the standpoint of consciousness—as it were, the zero point of two coordinates—that meanings, including those meanings we call values, are constituted. To be conscious of another center of consciousness is to be able in my own

61

acts of consciousness to take up the standpoint of that other. It implies the possibility of turning the other's "there" into my "here," or more generally, the possibility of a reciprocity of perspectives between two centers of consciousness. Yet I can never leave the frame of reference provided by my own consciousness, which is to say, my own way of orienting myself to the world, even in my attempts to take other centers of consciousness into account. Taking up the standpoint of the other can, therefore, only mean that I find some way to qualify my own acts of consciousness by an awareness of the other's specific orientation to the world. To achieve such a qualification, I have no recourse other than to interpret or perhaps intuit the meaning-constituting activity of the other center of consciousness on the basis of signs mediated by, or better, manifest in the bodily activity of that other. The other's acts of consciousness are apprehended in that bodily activity. That is to say, I immediately associate or "pair" certain perceived bodily acts with the activity of a center of consciousness like mine yet other than my own. Cf. Husserl, *Cartesian Meditations*, 108–15.

20. Levinas, *Totality and Infinity*, 51.

21. Ibid., 91ff.

22. Ibid., 118.

23. Ibid., 84.

24. Ibid., 73.

25. Ibid., 75.

26. Søren Kierkegaard, *Philosophical Fragments*, Eng. trans. David F. Swenson (Princeton: Princeton University Press, 1936), 5–16.

27. Cf. Kant, *Fundamental Principles of the Metaphysics of Morals*, 50. For a good treatment of Levinas's thought in relation to the moral philosophy of Kant, see Stephen G. Smith, *Levinas and Moral Reason* (M.A. thesis, Vanderbilt University, 1978), 1–73. Smith distinguishes the "rational" and the "reasonable." The reasonable, following Levinas, consists in shared understandings reached through discourse. The rational consists in the logical development of one's own maxims of action, in the sense of the Kantian categorical imperative. It is monological in contrast to the dialogical ethic opened up by Levinas.

28. Levinas, *Totality and Infinity*, 70ff.

29. Ibid., 244.

30. Ibid., 246.

31. On this point Friedrich Nietzsche correctly characterizes much popular Christian moral thought as a form of *resentment*. See, e.g., his *The Genealogy of Morals*, Eng. trans. Francis Golffing (Garden City, N.Y.: Doubleday & Co., Anchor Books, 1956), 116–69, 180–82, et al. Cf. Max Scheler's attempt to defend Christianity against Nietzsche's charge in his *Ressentiment*, Eng. trans. William W. Holdheim (New York: Schocken Books, 1972).

32. Levinas, *Totality and Infinity*, 213.

33. Cf. in this connection Paul Ramsey's discussion of the "neighbor-regarding care for the self" which is a feature in Christian love. Such care, he suggests, is not self-love at all. It is made up of "duties to the neighbor performed first upon the self." *Basic Christian Ethics* (New York: Charles Scribner's Sons, 1950), 159, 163.

34. This language points to a general theory of values as the proper context for interpreting moral values. For a preliminary sketch of such a theory, see chap. 3, "The Relation of Values to Human Need," in the present volume.

35. One might in this connection recall Erik H. Erikson's account of "Generativity" as a crucial accomplishment in the adult phase of the life cycle of the healthy personality. Erikson describes generativity as follows:

> Generativity is primarily the interest in establishing and guiding the next generation, although there are people who, from misfortune or because of special and genuine gifts in other directions, do not apply this drive to offspring but to other forms of altruistic concern and of creativity, which may absorb their kind of parental responsibility. The principal thing is to realize that this is a stage of the growth of the healthy personality and that where such enrichment fails altogether, regression from generativity to an obsessive need for pseudo intimacy takes place, often with a pervading sense of stagnation and interpersonal impoverishment. Individuals who do not develop generativity often begin to indulge themselves as if they were their own one and only child.

From "Growth and Crises of the Healthy Personality," *Psychological Issues* 1/1 (1959): 97.

3

THE RELATION OF VALUES
TO HUMAN NEED

"Good is a term which . . . must be applied," H. Richard Niebuhr has argued, "to that which meets the needs, which fits the capacity, which corresponds to the potentialities of an existant being. . . . Evil, on the other hand, is that which thwarts, destroys or starves a being in its activities."[1] Niebuhr correctly notes the connection between values and the gratification of human needs. Yet specifying the nature of that connection is a complex undertaking. The task of this essay is to trace some of those complexities so that the force of Niebuhr's basic insight might be strengthened and clarified.

On the one hand, values cannot be derived from a simple determination of the content of human needs and of the means for their efficient and maximal gratification. To know about certain needs and how to satisfy them is not in itself to know the value of such satisfaction; nor can the latter be grounded in the former in any direct and immediate fashion. The identification of values worthy of promotion through action is at least relatively independent of a description of the need-gratification processes present in human life.

On the other hand, values also cannot gain an immediate and direct grounding in a notion of reason, particularly if reason is understood with Kant in a purely formal and abstract sense.[2] Valuation does involve rational processes, but reason itself is conditioned and qualified. It is founded upon structures and processes which reflect the "belonging" of finite being to body, to a natural environment, to a social world, indeed, to the Ground of Being itself. These structures of "belonging" can be analyzed and interpreted as "needs," needs which must in some measure be gratified if concrete actors are to be able to function as moral agents at all.

At one level, these needs concern the conditions for the very possibility of acting, of the ability actors have to insert their purposes into the world through their own initiatives. The point could be stated as a proportion: the more complete the fulfillment of our needs as finite beings, the greater and the more diverse our powers of acting; the more we are deprived or frustrated in our quest to meet basic life requirements, the more we are limited and restricted in our possibilities of acting.

There is a deeper question, however, which belongs materially to valuation itself. Unless we are prepared to accept the idea that valuation, particularly moral valuation, implies our alienation from the conditions of our own being, and hence, a radical form of self-alienation, then our recognition of value and our loyalty to it in concrete action must in some appropriate fashion embrace and inform our interest in gratifying our own needs as finite beings.[3] To put the point somewhat differently, our ability to discern values and their claims upon our lives is essentially connected with a recognition of our own value as persons and with our hope that we shall find fulfillment at the deepest levels of our being. Thus, if valuation cannot be equated with the concern to gratify basic needs, it also cannot be isolated or abstracted from that concern.

These considerations permit a more precise statement of the central question. How is the apprehension of values to be understood so as to display both their essential and material connections with the gratification of basic human needs and also their distinctiveness as modalities of meaning which transcend and bestow significance upon such gratification?

Paul Ricoeur's studies in the philosophy of the will provide the primary resource for my treatment of this question, though Ricoeur's own work will be read in relation to the value theory of Max Scheler, to whom Ricoeur himself often looked for guidance in thinking about such matters.

Ricoeur does not venture a full-scale theory of values, particularly if such a theory includes a systematic, hierarchically organized presentation of values on the basis of which critical judgments might be made. In fact he gives little attention to value judgments as such except insofar as they are already encompassed in everyday deciding and acting. His principal interest is to provide an account of voluntary action, giving special attention to its rootage in the spontaneity of the body. A discussion of values enters into the picture chiefly because values prove to be essential ingredients in such action. Ricoeur's work is important, however, precisely for its portrayal of the presence of valuation, albeit latent or implicit, in the basic structures and dynamics of human deciding and acting. An account of these latent processes of valuation can clarify the material connections values have to the gratification of human need.

The essay falls into three major parts: the first two describe latent processes of valuation in everyday deciding and acting; the third shows how implicit values may become fully explicit. The first details latent valuation at work in everyday deciding and acting. The preponderance of attention is given to valuation at the "organic level." It is in the discussion of organically based needs and values that Ricoeur has worked out most fully his basic model of understanding. In the second part some suggestions are offered concerning the extension of this basic model to other levels and modalities of valuation.

The third part of the essay is rather schematic, though it too is essential to the analysis. Its function is to show how the latent valuation of everyday deciding and acting can become available for the self-conscious and critical value judgments of the reflective actor. To display the possibility of such judgments, it is necessary to establish the relative autonomy of values vis-à-vis the concrete gratification of human needs. The autonomy in question stems from the apriority of values, an apriority which, following Scheler, is taken to be not merely formal, but also material. The relative nature of this autonomy reflects the fact that values appear in the context of actions aimed at meeting human needs and hence are always colored by the perception of such needs.

LATENT VALUATION AT THE ORGANIC
LEVEL OF ACTION

Motives and Values

Ricoeur discusses the latent processes of valuation in an account of deciding and of the motives upon which it is based.[4] In deciding, Ricoeur suggests, I bind myself to implement in action a project which I entertain in my imagination. The project specifies that which I have in mind to do; it designates a future action to be carried out by me that is within my power. Every project, Ricoeur continues, has its reasons. These reasons make up the motive or motives upon which the project is based. The term "motive" often refers to the dynamics working in an actor which push or impel that actor to action. This interpretation is common in psychological studies of motivation. In Ricoeur's usage, however, motives are not taken in a causal sense. They consist in the reasons which justify a project, which give it a ground, a warrant, a legitimacy in the eyes of the actor. The reasons given may, to be sure, be spurious, a mere pretext for an action which has grounds of a quite different sort. Yet the fact that people often give spurious reasons for their chosen projects does not in any way count against the essential structural relation which links a project to its justifying motives. It simply means that the true motives for action are often concealed. Even so, every project has its reasons, its motives; motives give sense to the project as something worth doing.

By the same token, projects activate motives; they cast some possible motives for action into relief, permitting others to slip into the background. Our motives do not come to us in the form of a pre-established system with its well defined priorities and its qualifying conditions. They present themselves in a circular relation with the projects they justify. Consequently, to decide upon a project is at the same time to decide upon a pattern of motivation, upon a justifying basis for action. The two mutually require and condition each other.

It is in the motivation of a project that values appear. Motives constitute an implicit, pre-reflective valuation enveloped in the thrust of the project itself. To decide upon a project is to decide upon the values to be served and promoted by a particular action in a given situation. In some of his statements Ricoeur seems to equate motives and values so that one can mistakenly conclude that values have meaning only as concrete motives for action. Ricoeur does wish to challenge the notion that the cognition of values occurs apart from concrete human activity. Values are not timeless ideas even though they are exigencies which transcend immediate personal interests. Their appearance is tied to a history in which we actively collaborate, which we help invent. Motives "historialize" values, Ricoeur prefers to say. The fundamental relation in which valuation takes place is provided, therefore, by the motivation of a particular project.[5] Even so, a motive is not as such a value; it is a justifying reason or ground for a specific project. Ricoeur's language is carefully measured: values "appear" in the motivation of a project; they are "encountered," "recognized," or "discovered" in such motivation, but they are not created or invented by it. In some sense, therefore, values surpass motivation as such, and function to bestow a "seal" of approval upon its operation or to withhold that seal, as the case may be.

Needs and Motives

Whence comes the relative objectivity of values, their transcendence over concrete decisions for action and the motivating grounds for such decisions? Ricoeur opens his discussion of this question with an analysis of needs and their relation to motivation. For the most part, Ricoeur limits his discussion of these matters to organically based needs, making only passing reference to needs at other levels of experience—specifically the level of sociality. Indeed, the focus of his whole study is corporeality and its role in voluntary activity. Yet Ricoeur clearly recognizes the possibility of extending his analysis by analogy to other modalities of human need—especially to socially and culturally based needs.

The body, Ricoeur suggests, is the most fundamental source of motives and the revealer of a primordial layer of values: vital values.[6] To show how the body both gives rise to motives and also reveals values, Ricoeur offers a description of organically based needs in their relation to deciding. The prototype is provided by what might be called assimilative needs: needs for food, for fluids, perhaps also for sexual expression. Yet with variations, some of which Ricoeur elaborates, the structures which enable assimilative needs to enter into motivational processes are discernible in other types of vital needs, e.g., needs for security or for appropriate amounts of activity and rest.

Ricoeur's main interest is to show how organic needs become available to the will, to human deciding and acting. His claim is that needs and the objects of their gratification provide the *material* content of motives; motives in turn bestow *form* on these needs and their objects, shaping them into reasons which can serve to justify a given project or projects.[7] By means of this formula, Ricoeur both resists causal interpretations of the functioning of needs in human behavior and also acknowledges the prominence of need-gratification dynamics in the motivation of human action.

Needs "incline without necessity," Riceour contends.[8] They make up the "receptive" side of motivation. Receptivity does not imply passivity. Needs are "received" in motivation in a manner available to an active shaping. To make his point more precise, Ricoeur distinguishes in the structure of need both a "lack" of something and an "impetus" toward that which will fill up the lack. The "lack" is involuntary; it confronts us with a given, a necessity, stemming from our bodily existence and its structure of belonging to its environment. The "impetus" is, however, in our control. I cannot help being hungry; but I can persist in my fast provided my reasons for doing so have sufficient weight in my consciousness. Needs refer themselves to the will, therefore, in the form of motives.

Imagination, Needs, and Motives

How does the material of human needs get "informed" into motives? Ricoeur's answer is provided in an account of the role imagination plays in willing. Imagination mediates between the "matter" of need and the "form" of motive, rendering corporeal spontaneity available to voluntary direction.

Imagination follows perception. It cannot operate except with materials already given to experience. In this context the relevant experience is one of having a need gratified: experiencing the eating of food as relieving the pangs of hunger, experiencing orgasmic release as dissipating accumulated sexual tensions in the body. Apart from experiences of gratification of a concrete sort, needs remain "blind," mere indicators of a "vaguely oriented distress."[9] Need-gratification experiences serve to clarify needs, to display to consciousness their import for the being of the actor. In this respect an account of needs cannot strictly speaking explain behavior aimed at their gratification. The concrete means for meeting the needs in question are already given in experience prior to the full disclosure of the needs themselves.

In practice, our needs and the appropriate ways of dealing with them are shaped in large measure by cultural definitions of value and of normative patterns of behavior. Through complex processes of socialization, we internalize these cultural definitions into our individual self-understandings.[10]

On the basis of previous experience or previous socially mediated learnings, we respond to the visceral distress of "lack" by representing to ourselves in the imagination: (1) that object or process which will relieve the distress, and (2) possible ways of acting that will give us access to such relief. Imagination allows us to break out of the blind necessity of visceral drives. It gives us distance from the immediacy of experience so that we can play a shaping role in that experience. It enables us to exercise some conscious direction over the course of our lives through the adoption of projects for our future actions which reflect our own preferred motives in various situations.

Imagination, Needs, and Values

To sum up the discussion thus far, needs enter into motivation as the "matter" of motives. Motives in turn "form" our needs into reasons capable of justifying our chosen courses of action. Imagination plays the mediating role, presenting to the will representations of possible ways of gratifying felt needs. The next task is to make explicit the import of this account for clarifying the presence of values in human experience.

Ricoeur emphasizes the fact that values "appear" in the motivation of specific projects, not in some abstract or purely theoretical process of reflection. At the same time, he notes, we do not create or invent values in the motivation of our projects; we rather discover them, encounter them, come to acknowledge and respect them. Thus, values have a certain independence of the motivation of projects even though they concretely appear to consciousness only in relation to such motivation. What are the grounds for that independence? How does an account of human needs and the modes of their gratification relate to those grounds?

Ricoeur apparently sees a close connection between needs and values, for he describes the relation of needs to motives in a manner analogous to his earlier formulae regarding the relation of motives and values. We do not invent our needs or the conditions of their gratification, he notes. We discover them, encounter them, and learn means of dealing with them. Needs apparently transcend motives, therefore, as the pre-given matter of motive, requiring only to be historialized in concrete decisions in order to provide the justifying grounds of action. Is the relative objectivity of needs vis-à-vis motives also the clue to the transcendence of values over the motivation of particular projects? Though Ricoeur is seeking to establish an essential connection between needs and values, he is in no case simply equating values with that which meets our needs, nor with a character or quality of the objects, activities, or relations which gratify our needs. What then is this connection?

Values appear or emerge *through* needs, Ricoeur claims, even though I as generator of my acts have not posited them.[11] One could expand this formula: values appear *in* motivation *by means of needs*. But precisely how do they appear? Ricoeur's answer in *The Voluntary and the Involuntary* is somewhat obscure. He resorts to examples, suggesting an immediate apprehension of value founded on corporeality: "Bread is good, wine is good." "Before I will," he continues, "I am already solicited by a value by virtue of the fact that I exist in the flesh."[12] But what is meant by these examples? Is bread as such—considered as a concrete object—properly to be called a value? Is it not more appropriate to call it a concrete good or at least a concrete kind of good?[13] But if bread is a particular good and not a value as such, to what does the term "value" refer? To certain *qualities* possessed by the bread, for example, its agreeable taste or its suitability for assuaging our hunger, for giving us energy, for meeting some of our nutritional requirements? And how do we come to acknowledge such qualities and their claims upon our regard?

Ricoeur's view seems to be that the latent valuation implied in the motivation of a project is directed in the first instance not toward values as such, but toward concrete goods, relations, and processes. Values are ingredient in these goods. Indeed, the goodness of the goods is based upon the values they embody, but the values themselves remain largely latent in those goods. They have not yet been brought clearly into view. We are still left with the task of describing how such meanings manifest themselves to consciousness; more importantly, of uncovering the manner in which they bear to the actor the specific sense of "value." I will subsequently return to this point. In the present context, however, Ricoeur is not yet dealing with value judgments per se. He is rather attending to latent processes of valuation which are enfolded in the motivation of projects. To say that values (in the latent or pre-reflective sense) appear by means of need apparently means that I experience the concrete realities which meet my needs as goods in which values are ingredient. Bread satisfies my hunger. Wine quenches my thirst. To return to Ricoeur's earlier point, we could say that our fleshly existence is the primal occasion which opens us to solicitation by the use-values enfolded in the concrete goods, bread and wine.

The Affective Disclosure of Value: Pleasure

The next task is to make more explicit the modalities of this value solicitation. What aspects of need-gratification experiences function to disclose the value signification of the goods which provide the gratification? Ricoeur's answer centers in an account of pleasure as a revealer of value.

The "pure" function of pleasure, Ricoeur suggests, is to present an entity as *good* at the same time that perception presents it as real. Pleasure is not autonomous. It is rather an index which discloses a need in the process of being satisfied. To be sure, it is possible to pursue pleasure for its own sake, but then pleasure is faulted, a "cut and already fading flower." Originally, pleasure is secondary with respect to need. It is the penultimate phase of the need cycle, the final phase being one of possession and enjoyment. Pleasure aims at enjoyment. It is in transition from lack to satisfaction.

How does pleasure enter into motivational processes? As in the case of his earlier discussion of needs, Ricoeur points to the role of imagination. Through imagination the concrete experiences of pleasure in past actions become the basis for an anticipation of pleasure to be gained by means of possible future actions. This anticipation is not simply a formal orientation of consciousness toward an expected future, a knowledge of the experiences that will likely accompany particular actions. It is enlivened by a material image which is itself a representation, an analogon, of future pleasure. That is to say, I do not simply know that the roast turkey will be good. I can almost taste it even now. I have a present, affective image of what the eating will be like.

Just as the experience of pleasure is secondary to the gratification of need, so also the anticipation of pleasure is secondary to the imaginative representation of that object, process, event, or relation which will gratify need. One could say that the anticipation of pleasure is represented *on* the imagined objects or processes that will meet our needs. Thus imagination represents to consciousness: (1) an absent object which will meet a need (bread, wine); (2) ways of gaining access to that object; and (3) anticipated feelings—the image of pleasure and the imaginary apprehension of future pleasure—which disclose to the subject the value of that absent object. It is the expectation of pleasure which uncovers overtones of value in the pure representation of absence; it attests the belonging of need to the sphere of valuation.

Ricoeur names the anticipation of pleasure "desire." Desire is the present experience of need as lack and as urge, extended by the representation of the absent object that will fill up the lack and by the imaginative anticipation of the pleasure which will accompany the gratification of the need. The anticipation of pleasure amounts to a latent valuation. To anticipate pleasure is to be ready to say: This is good. Yet the affective intention of pleasure-to-be is still not as such an explicit value judgment.

Summary and Conclusion

I have been describing the latent processes of valuation which are present in deciding and acting. According to this account, values appear in the motivation of a project. Their significance for human life is thus inseparably linked to human action, more specifically, to the justifying grounds of action. Moreover, values appear by means of need, presumably as the immanent and latent ground of the goodness of the things, processes, or relations which function to gratify human needs. Further, the value significance of these concrete "goods" which satisfy human needs becomes manifest in the experience of pleasure. Pleasure is the affective index disclosing the fact that needs are on the way to gratification. Finally, imagination is the middle term in this process. It connects the "matter" of need and its gratification, including the pleasure which accompanies such gratification, with the "form" of the motive as the justifying ground of a particular project of human action. The next task is to extend this basic model to other levels and modalities of human action.

IMPLICIT VALUATION AT OTHER LEVELS OF ACTION

Steps in the Completion of the Value Theory

What is involved in completing this account of values and their relations to human needs? Three steps are crucial.

(1) I have sketched the latent processes of valuation at work in the self's need-gratification activity at the organic level. Even at this level, I have attended only to positive assimilative needs, chiefly, needs for food and for drink. The next step is to extend this basic model, with appropriate adjustments and alterations, to the other principal areas of human need and of need-gratification activity. Through such an extension we can begin to identify the multiplicity and heterogeneity of values which appear to us by way of diverse types of human need. We bring into view the whole range of value experiences in their pre-reflective forms.

(2) I have noted that valuation in its pre-reflective expressions is oriented not to values as such, but to concrete goods which serve to gratify human needs. It remains to determine the operations through which the value meanings ingredient in these concrete goods become explicit. Ricoeur suggests that a kind of practical "reduction" (in the phenomenological sense), effected on the concrete goods, is necessary in order to set in relief the meanings which are properly to be called "values." Following Max Scheler, he believes that this reduction can bring to light an *a priori* value realm. He also broadly shares Scheler's view that the cognitive mode appropriate to this value realm is predominantly affective. More strongly than Scheler, however, he stresses the connection between the affective cognition of values and concrete experiences of need-gratification. Reducing to their value meanings of the concrete goods encountered in need-gratification activities renders implicit experiences of value available to self-conscious and critical value judgments.

(3) Finally, value judgments imply acts of ranking or preferring among the multiplicity of values appearing to consciousness in various life situations. The discussion of the value realm gains completion, therefore, in an account of preferring as it bears upon

the values we recognize and hold in honor. To what extent does value-ranking itself have an *a priori* base? To what extent is it relative to a particular history or cultural tradition? To what extent is it purely subjective, accidental, arbitrary, even capricious?

Each of these steps is exceedingly complex in itself. It is not possible in a brief study to give a satisfactory account of any one of them. It is my intent simply to suggest what they entail, why they are important, and how they might complete the more detailed description of latent valuation contained in the first section of the chapter.

Implicit Valuation at the Level of History

In examining the voluntary-involuntary dialectic Ricoeur's special interest is to highlight the meaning of body in human deciding and acting. Consequently, the role played by organic needs in the apprehension of values receives extensive attention. At the same time, Ricoeur acknowledges other basic levels of valuation which are amenable to analysis in terms of the model developed for the organic level. Two such levels are treated in *The Voluntary and the Involuntary*. Ricoeur identifies the first of these as the level of history. History chiefly concerns the social context of motivation and valuation. The body is also involved in this level of valuation. Indeed, it plays a role in the apprehension of all motives and, through them, all values whatever. Thus, no values can reach us nor motives incline us which do not impress our sensibilities.[14] Even so, the social context brings into play motives and values not present at the organic level: those related to our existence as social beings.

The language of need, Ricoeur shows, is applicable to an analysis of human sociality and its implicit values. We lack something other than bread and water. We also lack the "other" and his or her good. By myself I am empty. It is the other like me who completes me in my social and personal being, just as food completes me in my being as body.[15] The other is necessary for me because selfhood is itself fundamentally intersubjective. The self has no isolated being; it is being-in-common-with-others. Thus, I have need for others in the constitution of my own being as person.

At this point, the specifically moral element enters into Ricoeur's discussion of the latent modalities of valuation. I not only need and desire "others" and their fellowship; I become "obligated" to them. I discover that they matter alongside of me: their needs count as mine; their opinions proceed from a center of perspective and valuation having a dignity comparable to my own. If I am to enjoy community with others, community I need and desire for the completion of my own being, I must acknowledge and take up my own obligation to them. I must respect their dignity and promote their well-being. Only by fulfilling these obligations, at least to a minimal degree, can I participate in the community I require as a condition of my own selfhood. The values emerging by means of needs implicit in the self's intersubjective constitution can be promoted only by an acceptance and fulfillment of reciprocal obligations to the significant others involved in those transactions. Given the centrality of intersubjectivity in the formation and maintenance of selfhood, it is not surprising that the dialectic between need for the other and obligation to that other, which is characteristic of value experience at this level, should become a basic paradigm for the interpretation of moral experience.[16]

Ricoeur calls attention to the ways in which body penetrates the milieu of history and of human sociality. He might just as appropriately have stressed the intersubjectivity of body, that is, the permeation of corporeal spontaneity by human sociality and historicity. The interpenetration of value levels means that there can be no values which are purely corporeal or purely intersubjective. Since these modalities of value are fundamental to the constitution of selfhood, they always manifest themselves in ways that are mutually limiting and conditioning.

Implicit Valuation and the Problem of Consent
In *The Voluntary and the Involuntary* Ricoeur explicitly speaks of only two levels of value: the organic and the historical. These levels in their interrelationships, he suggests, present the central and decisive problems for the moral life. They surface the anguish we experience when our own survival and well-being come into conflict with the vital needs and interests of others. Nonetheless, Ricoeur discusses another stratum of experiences which can be understood as a third level of value. This level of valuation manifests dynamics analogous to those present in the corporeal and social dimensions of experience. It concerns the

self's basic stance toward the meaning and value of being as such. Ricoeur speaks of it in terms of the problem of consent, that is, the necessity of adopting some attitude toward the inescapable limits and unalterable givens which surround and condition the voluntary activity of human actors: matters of personal temperament, the operation of the unconscious, the strange contingency of birth and death.

Ricoeur does not use the category of need or of need-gratification to talk about this level of experience. Yet the idea is present. In addition to those insistent drives and life requisites which are significantly amenable to our active shaping and control, we also confront, Ricoeur argues, elements of necessity which seem to be fundamentally beyond our voluntary direction, and hence beyond even the possibility of our personal and responsible appropriation. Such necessity can threaten us as an alien surd. It has the potential to undermine the allure and immediate self-evidence of values which manifest themselves at other levels of experience. That is to say, if being itself is ultimately meaningless and valueless, then perhaps human life and human community are likewise without meaning and value, at least when they involve great difficulty, conflict, and pain. If our commitments to promote other modalities of value are to be more than fragmentary and equivocal, we must have some means of coming to terms positively with this final limit to human willing.

At this level the appearance of values takes on a peculiarly religious flavor. One could say that human beings have a need to discern and affirm the meaning and value of being at the level of ultimacy in order to be fully functioning selves. Apart from at least a partial or perhaps fragmentary gratification of this need, the satisfaction of other modalities of need becomes problematic and equivocal.

Ricoeur does not deal directly with the latent indications of valuation which are present in the need to consent in some global sense to the goodness of the necessity in being. He rather provides a comparison among some selected modalities of consent which have been important in Western culture: stoic, orphic, and eschatological. And these options in no sense exhaust the possibilities. Stoic consent, he argues, is imperfect, for it achieves its accommodation to necessity by a rational detachment which denies the self's feelings and passions. Orphic consent in contrast is hyperbolic; it finally loses the self completely in an ecstatic and exhilarating admiration of being which dissolves all particularity. Ricoeur finds the eschatological mode of consent, which is characteristic of biblical faith, to be the most profoundly nuanced of these three. It unites the orphic admiration of being with an affirmation of self which is more embracing than stoic apathy. At the same time, it addresses the awful reality of human evil, calling us, for the sake of the anticipated new heaven and new earth, to consent in hope to what is given to us—in spite of its distortions and brokenness. Eschatological consent, Ricoeur suggests, is the will to convert all hostility into a fraternal tension within the unity of creation.[17]

Ricoeur continues to deal with the problem of consent in subsequent writings. In *Fallible Man* he associates it with the idea of happiness (see especially his discussion of "affective fragility").[18] In *The Symbolism of Evil*, consent shows itself in Ricoeur's interpretation of great myths of evil in Western culture: the cosmogonic (Babylonian and Sumerian), the gnostic (Hellenistic), the tragic (Greek), and the Adamic (Hebraic-Christian). In this discussion, however, it is not simply experienced necessity which makes consent difficult, but the absurd contingency of human evil; not only the involuntary, but the self-enslavement of the voluntary. The function of these classic myths is to render evil sufficiently intelligible so that being, despite its manifest ambiguity, might yet be affirmed as good. Of these four, the Adamic myth gains preeminence in the comparison, primarily because of its subtlety in joining the inwardness and voluntariness of human responsibility for evil with the tragic elements of evil, those elements which repeatedly overwhelm the will.[19] This myth, especially in its christological development, captures the eschatological structure of consent previously highlighted in *The Voluntary and the Involuntary*.

More recently, Ricoeur has taken up the same theme in expounding further the link in Christian understanding between unjustifiable evil and reconciliation in the sacred.[20] Consent in this discussion is expressed as an "in spite of," a "thanks to," and a "how much more." It consists in a reconciliation which occurs *in spite of* evil; it takes place *thanks to* One who brings good out of evil; it involves a "strange logic of superabundance," so that "where sin increased, grace abounded all the more" (Rom.

5:21). Here too echoes of Ricoeur's initial discussion in *The Voluntary and the Involuntary* are present, modified by the inclusion of an account of evil and its defeat.

What is striking about these discussions is that the latent valuation of being, taken in the sense of ultimacy, does not in Ricoeur's view normally manifest itself immediately and directly in the motivation of concrete action. Normally it shows itself in what Ricoeur likes to call the "fullness of language," in symbol, myth, and metaphor. Symbols and myths express and shape our perceptions of the fundamental meaning and value of being at pre-reflective levels of experience. We gain access to the valuative processes they embody through hermeneutic operations rather than through a phenomenological description of deciding and acting.

To be sure, religious meanings can motivate specific actions. Explicit cultic and devotional acts would, for example, seem to be religiously motivated in a direct sense. Likewise, religious motivations would bear immediately upon decisions involving a choice between apostasy and martyrdom. In such decisions nothing less than the ultimate meaning of our existence as concrete selves is at stake. For the most part, however, the linguistic expressions embodying the specific modality of our consent to being do not directly affect the motivation of discrete and concrete decisions and actions. They rather define the "horizon" of value which orders and bestows significance upon the more specific and limited values appearing in the motivation of particular projects. As is widely acknowledged in theological ethics, this horizon has a material bearing on the evaluation of concrete actions, yet that bearing is rarely exact or precise. It can set some limits to action; it also suggests certain basic attitudes, interests, and directions as important ingredients in all action. Yet, except in special circumstances, it does not move to the foreground as the decisive determinant of a particular action.

Summary and Conclusion

To sum up, Ricoeur's thought gives us access to at least three distinguishable levels of motivation and valuation: the organic, the social-historical, and the religious or ultimate (consent). Each of these is amenable to analysis in terms of needs and need gratification. Each involves certain modalities of feeling in the latent apprehension of value: pleasure, satisfaction, contentment, joy, wonder, or awe. Each is linked to positive affective experiences that reveal the presence of value in concrete goods in a way that can become available for concrete value judgments.[21]

RENDERING VALUES EXPLICIT

"Reducing" Concrete Goods to Their A Priori Value Essences

How do the instances of latent valuation take on an explicit value meaning of the sort that is implied in value judgments? In *Fallible Man* Ricoeur suggests that values become explicit by means of a "reduction" effected on the concrete goods which serve to gratify our needs. Ricoeur does not elaborate this suggestion, nor does he carry out the sorts of operations it might involve. But he does offer some hints which can assist us in setting forth the movement from implicit valuation to explicit value judgments.

In tracing the appearance of values, we attend preeminently to what is given in experience. We do not begin with the explicit value language which is already a part of our cultural inheritance. This language is, of course, quite important. It normally shapes the way we think about values. Under the influence of Martin Heidegger and Hans-Georg Gadamer, Ricoeur himself later places considerable weight on the fact that language, as operative in a culture and its literature, gives us a world. Only in and through language, that is to say, are we able to apprehend and articulate as a meaningful whole what is present to experience.[22] This insight helps us understand the significance of value language for our experience of value. In his earlier thought about values, however, Ricoeur's accent is on our concrete experiences of those objects, processes, and relations that have been disclosed to us as good by means of positive affects of various kinds: agreeable sensations, pleasure, feelings of vigor and well-being. This accent dramatizes the ingredient of values in our ordinary activities. It also establishes the possibility that experience might provide us with resources for critical thinking about well-established, socially sanctioned value traditions.

Initially, therefore, an inquiry into the genesis of explicit value judgments must follow the direction indicated by those positive affects which accompany need-gratification experiences. We ask what these affects disclose to us about the realities we encounter.

We seek to comprehend the sense or meaning, borne by those realities, which corresponds to the affects. The affects are taken in their intentional significance, as participating in the basic orientation of consciousness to that of which it is conscious. They are not merely indices of subjective states; they function in the first instance to reveal a certain kind of meaning. This meaning interprets for us why and in what respects the realities we encounter are important. In Ricoeur's vivid expressions: such meaning displays our "complicity" in the world, our "inherence" in it, our "belonging" to it.[23] Elaborating this suggestion, Ricoeur speaks of the dialectic which holds between knowing and feeling. Knowing distances us from the world while feeling relates us to it. More precisely, percepts present to us as *real* the objects and processes we encounter, and feeling discloses them as *significant*. Percepts and affects occur together in concrete experience, though they order such experience in contrasting ways. Actually feeling already has a double reference in itself. It links us, on the one hand, to those facets of worldy realities which bear their value for us; in this respect it has an outward movement, an objective thrust. On the other hand, it reveals the intimacy of our involvement with those realities; it calls attention to their impact on us. In this respect, it has an inward movement, a subjective thrust.[24] In sum, feelings tell of our "elective harmonies and disharmonies with realities whose affective image we carry in ourselves in the mode of 'good' or 'bad.'"[25] Values are meanings which articulate and render intelligible the understandings these feelings betray.

The attempt to make explicit the values disclosed by particular affects is by no means a simple undertaking, chiefly because concrete realities cannot be reduced to a single value meaning, perhaps not even to an identifiable value grouping (e.g., organic values). Here we discover in a new fashion what Edmund Husserl in his studies of perception called the *horizonal* character of the world.[26] The perceived meanings we "fix" in consciousness, he notes, always bear with them open possibilities for further perceptions of a related but different sort. This open horizon is already manifest in the elemental fact that a perceived object continually presents to us new facets as we move around it. These facets will either confirm our prior expectations or surprise us with the unexpected. The same horizonal structure orders our discernment of values, though with a much richer, more variegated set of possibilities. Thus, any value we might be able to isolate as a feature in the significance of a given reality can at most articulate only one facet of that significance. Other possibilities continuously hover before any single value apprehension. Indeed, discerning a single value may itself activate and bring into awareness a whole range of associated values, disclosing the complexity of experience.

A meeting between lovers, e.g., brings into play an abundance of values too rich and complex for the most extensive account: those residing in the surface sensations of sexual excitement, those present in the deep and encompassing sense of well-being which spreads out over the entire body with the occurrence of orgasm; those expressing the closeness two vulnerable beings feel for each other; those articulating long-term commitments and loyalties, or perhaps the wonder of a new love; those linked to the experiences two persons have of growing older together, through good times and bad, through crises and their resolution, through the ceaseless rhythm of distance and closeness, alienation and renewed intimacy. It would be absurd to ask about *the* value of such a meeting, or even about its *essential* or primary value. Any single articulation of its value would in part be a function of the guiding interest at work at a given moment. Indeed, concrete experiences not only bear a multiplicity of value meanings; they characteristically present values in conflict. This conflict is manifest in feelings of ambivalence concerning the realities in question. And such ambivalence may also lead to equivocation in decision making, and to half-heartedness in carrying out our decisions in subsequent actions.

The central point to make is that values are particular kinds of meanings. They convey the significance-for-us of the realities we encounter in the world. These meanings are not immediately given to us. Immediately given are the concrete objects, processes and relations which figure in our day-to-day activities. Value meanings reside in these realities. It is only through a reflective effort, guided by the relevant affects, that we are able to bring them explicitly into view. If we are successful in this undertaking, we arrive at something akin to an *original recognition* of those qualities which account for the significance various realities have in the economy of our being. These qualities take on a certain authority in our lives; they make particular claims upon us in our deliberations, all the more so as we mature in our understanding and appreciation of the values which inform our lives.

On the basis of this account, one can with Ricoeur speak of an *a priori* realm of values.[27] The values discerned are not to be understood as merely subjective or arbitrary expressions of ways of looking at things, a personal valuation added to or imposed upon the essentially value-neutral material of experience. Value is constitutive of experience, of our relations with persons and things. Phenomenology simply provides a way of describing how these value elements come into view. Ricoeur properly notes: we do not invent values; we discover them and come to acknowledge them in the course of our experience. Moreover, value meanings are not the same things as motives and needs even though they appear in motivation by means of needs. In themselves they are relatively independent of and prior to concrete motivation and concrete patterns of need-gratification. As I have indicated, they function to bestow a seal of approval on our motives, or perhaps to withhold that seal for the sake of higher values. Nonetheless, values do not appear except in relation to concrete human commitments, concrete decisions and actions, which themselves reflect various modalities of need-gratification activity. The discernment of values is bound up with the unfolding of a history in which we participate.

This analysis permits us to reformulate the comments of H. Richard Niebuhr which were cited at the beginning. Niebuhr's identification of the good with that which meets the needs, fits the capacity, and corresponds to the potentialities of an existent being, captures Ricoeur's insistence on the historialization of values in concrete goods. It calls attention to the fact that values appear by means of needs in the motivation of specific projects. However, Niebuhr has not stated so clearly the independence of value-type meanings from accounts of the needs of actual beings and the possible ways of meeting those needs. He obscures, in other words, the apriority of values which enables us to see values in actions aimed at furthering a being's realization of its own distinctive tendencies. Ricoeur keeps in view the distinction between value-type meanings and other kinds of meanings—motives, needs, positive affective experiences—but he does so without losing sight of the essential connection values have to human needs and their gratification.

A Priori Value Preferences

One final step is necessary to complete this account of the appearance of values in relation to human need. It belongs to the meaning of value judgments to rank or order values, to prefer some value or values over others. Any value is absolute in its claims so long as it remains uncontested. It is the presence in experience of multiple and heterogenous values that requires of us some comparing and weighing among the values we recognize and would promote by our actions. Deciding among possible projects of action in itself involves establishing value priorities in a given situation. In fact, we would not have any cause to render value meanings explicit if we did not face the necessity of making choices among action possibilities. That necessity presses us to isolate and rank the values likely to be served by competing action projects. The problem is to determine the grounds for such ranking.

For the most part the specific value rankings that govern our life patterns are borne by the cultures into which we have been socialized, modified by particular features in our individual life histories. They are functions of the ways in which we have worked out our personal identities in the context of a structured set of socially shared value-orientations. In this respect they are relative to particular societies and to personal life plans. There is, as a result, a good deal of historical variation in the value patterns acknowledged and honored by human beings. Even so, all societies and all individual actors have need of fairly stable value rankings as a reference for decisions and actions. Otherwise, the preferring which belongs to value judgments would lack a reliable basis.[28]

Can we also identify an a priori value hierarchy? Are some values intrinsically superior to others? Are there any patterns in value relations that belong to value meanings as such? And if there are such patterns, in what manner do they limit and structure the range of variations possible in human value preferences? On these questions I am in no position to say anything definitive. I can only offer some brief suggestions which might merit further consideration.

To begin with, any a priori value pattern we might be able to uncover would bear some relation to basic human needs and the means of their gratification. Such is at least the guiding thread of this study. Thus, we might in any setting anticipate value clusters around such things as food and drink, physical shelter, exercise and rest, sexuality. Similarly, we might expect a socially sanctioned regard for a normative order capable of directing and constraining human interactions, specifying what is required and what is prohibited, what is desired and what is permitted, as a way of protecting and nurturing the well-being of the members of the society. We might also look for some definition of appropriate responses to those ultimate "necessities" which mark human finitude, especially birth and death. With these remarks I am, of course, simply recalling the principal value clusters isolated by Ricoeur in his discussion of deciding and acting. Each of these clusters would be open to considerable elaboration in a fully developed value theory.

Acknowledging the a priori status of value meanings of these sorts does not by any means imply approval of all their various articulations in human societies. In terms of our own particular commitments, for example, we may find the following phenomena coexistent in the dominant values of a given society: a surplus repression of instinctual energies, unacceptable differentials in basic human life chances, insufficient regard for social solidarity among human beings, shocking exploitation of some persons by others, carelessness toward the natural environment, and an idolatrous confusion of creaturely goods with the ultimately real. Nonetheless, we are not likely to find either persons or societies which do not honor some version of these basic value types. They are too closely linked to those "elective harmonies and disharmonies" which make up our worldly being for us to disregard them altogether. As such, they enable us to organize our quest for appropriate normative values.

I suspect that we can go beyond the simple recognition of basic value clusters. We can also inquire into the underlying unity of each. We can seek to discern those superordinate or encompassing value meanings in each value cluster which bestow significance upon the multiplicity of discrete values in the cluster. Thus, despite their multiplicity and heterogeneity, the various organic values—nutrition, security, exercise, rest, sexual gratification—all gain their unity and their fuller meaning by way of the more fundamental value of life itself, interpreted in this instance solely with reference to bodily strength and vigor. When faced with death, Ricoeur observes, my "being in life" suddenly draws together all the meanings associated with my corporeality.[29] In this respect "life" emerges as an a priori value essence which displays what is at stake in the concrete goods that protect, nourish, sustain, and express life in the activities of actual beings.

Similarly, there is implicit in social-historical values a recognition, among other things, of an obligatory moral order. Ricoeur uses the term "justice" to indicate this order. It specifies principles for balancing the claims various individuals make on collective recources and for distributing the burdens which must be borne in the interest of social viability and effectiveness. A moral order is an essential constituent in the concrete good of human communities. Actually it may be more correct to speak of justice not as a substantive value in itself, but as a moral norm which regulates human action. This norm then derives its authority from the more fundamental apprehension of the value of persons and personal community.

Finally, implicit in the patterns of consent, which express human attitudes towards experienced necessity, is a manner of imaging what is taken to be ultimately real, and a sense of the positive and negative bearing of that real upon the human quest for the fullness of being. For monotheistic understandings, the essential identity of being and value comes into view at this point: whatever is, is good!

If we are able in some such fashion to uncover a limited number of encompassing value meanings in the various value clusters, we will have moved a long way toward simplifying the resources for critical value judgments that are provided by our concrete experiences of value. Such notions will not permit a direct resolution of the value conflicts confronted in actual decision making. But they will assist us in orienting ourselves more appropriately to those conflicts.

Can we take the analysis one step further? Can we speak of a priori rankings among value clusters, particularly the three singled out in Ricoeur's philosophy of the will? Ricoeur's discussion of "affective fragility" in *Fallible Man* sheds light on this question.[30] His immediate aim in this discussion is to set forth the structural basis of human vulnerability to evil. That vulnerability, he suggests, can be seen in the fact that our affective responses to the world are stretched out between finite and infinite poles of experience. Some affects are more or less finite and limited, e.g., pleasurable sensations accompanying the gratification of organic needs (*epithymia* or desire); others are infinite and all-embracing, in particular the anticipatory experiences of blessedness or joy which accompany our "consent" to being (*eros* or aspiration after the ultimate good); still others lie between these poles, manifesting their tension in a singularly significant fashion, e.g., the zeal for fame or power or possessions (*thumos* or passion).

Our vulnerability to evil stems from the extraordinary difficulty of maintaining in a proper balance these polar tendencies in our affective life. We are tempted, on the one hand, to invest finite bodily pleasures with the infinite meanings expressed by the term "blessedness." We yield to this temptation in seeking the fulfillment of our being through the maximization of pleasurable experiences at the expense of all other considerations. On the other hand, for the sake of authentically spiritual values we may be tempted to overleap our finitude and in so doing conceal from ourselves our essential "belonging" to body and to world. We yield to this temptation in exalting unduly our radical freedom with respect to our bodies, lapsing into fanaticism and self-righteousness, condemning and perhaps even actively attempting to suppress and control others who do not share our value commitments. The mediating passions carry a double temptation: to flee in anxiety from one's self-transcending possibilities, and to exalt oneself arrogantly in a fashion that amounts to a refusal of finitude.

The mediating passions are especially important because of their intimate association with self-experience. They are also especially ambiguous, as the terms "power," "property," and "honor" suggest. Each designates a legitimate aspect of selfhood; yet each is subject to destructive distortions. Thus, power becomes domination, not competence or effectiveness; property becomes a means of self-expansion, resulting in the violation of others, not a legitimate accompaniment of one's being as body; and honor becomes haughtiness, not a proper sense of dignity and self-worth. Or alternatively, to avoid the risks of dominance,

one is passive, submissive, fleeing responsibility; to avoid ob-
session with possessions, one denies a proper sense of "mine-
ness" as a feature of worldly being; and to avoid arrogance, one
lapses into self-hatred.[31]

How does this treatment of affective fragility link up with the
quest for an a priori value hierarchy? The key point is to recall
that feelings are *revealers* of value. They are not ends in themselves. Corresponding to the three basic types of affectivity,
therefore, are three modalities of value. Epithymia or desire discloses organic values; eros or aspiration brings into view values
linked to consent, a sense of the ultimate unity of being and
value; and thumos or passion attests social-historical values. The
experience of value, that is to say, itself reflects and participates
in the fragility of feeling. It too is wholly bound up with human
vulnerability to evil.

We do see in this discussion some changes in Ricoeur's characterization of the social-historical value realm. Instead of speaking of the decentering of perspective effected on value experience by the presence of the other, or of justice as a normative
order regulating human interactions, we find an account of the
dynamics of self-experience. However, these two discussions are
clearly complementary: the latter concerns the potentialities
given with personal existence; the former highlights the importance of other persons—their dignity as centers of meaning and
value—in counterpoint to the impulses of my own being. Justice,
we could say, structures and regulates human interests in possessions, power, and honor. It brings before each of us the claims
of others, comparable in weight to our own, for personal fulfillment. Yet both of these readings of social-historical values finally
derive their authority from the more elemental recognition of the
value of persons and personal community.[32]

Guided by the portrayal of affective fragility, we have a means
of thinking about priority relations among the principal value
clusters. The value clusters are ordered around a polar tension
which reflects the distinctively human way of being in the world.
Ricoeur describes this tension in terms of a finite-infinite dialectic. The term infinite is not altogether apt. Even in our self-
transcendence, in our openness to the sacred, we remain through
and through finite. Yet we are able indefinitely to surpass any
concrete actualizations of our being. This capacity at least pro-

vides us with a negative idea of infinity.[33] In terms of the finite-infinite dialectic we can speak of organic values as situated near the finite pole of value experience, that is, in their most appropriate realizations. Ideally, they remain quite particular and singular in their claims. Spiritual values in contrast are situated near the infinite pole. They bring into view our thrust toward totality, toward completion. In this respect, they attest our openness to the ultimate, the holy, and to the radical freedom such openness implies. They are also most acutely subject to demonic distortions in the human quest for what is perceived to be the good. Social-historical values lie in between the organic and the spiritual. And yet they are not actually in between. As the most distinctively human values, they participate dialectically in the two primary value poles. In this respect they enable us to thematize the unity of value experience, just as they manifest most clearly its ambiguity.[34]

By portraying value relations in a polar pattern, we gain a number of advantages over the more typical image of value strata stacked one on top of the other, the image which actually conforms most closely to the notion of a hierarchy.[35] We are able to appreciate and conceptualize human vulnerability to evil. We are able to represent the interpenetration of distinguishable value modalities, for example, that vital values enter substantively into peculiarly social or moral ones, conditioning and qualifying them, and vice versa. We can take account of the fact that values which are "lower" in a general ranking may and often do enjoy priority in given instances of concrete deciding and acting. Yet we are able to accomplish this goal without obscuring the fact that there are ranks among value types. Thus, though contingent circumstances may profoundly affect concrete priorities, it is normally the case that (1) personal integrity and self-esteem are more to be valued than the inventively nuanced gratification of physiological needs; (2) personal integrity and self-esteem themselves depend for their value upon the deeper values of intimacy and mutual caring characteristic of rich, human community; and (3) all of these modalities of value experience ultimately gain their significance only with reference to concrete disclosures and symbolizations of the meaning and value of being itself.

Actually the relation of lower and higher values is more complex still. We can distinguish two kinds of priority in the ranking of values: a priority of *conditions* and a priority of *meanings*. The lower values take priority in the former sense, for their relative actualization in human life is itself a precondition for the possibility of the appearance to consciousness of the higher values. The higher values in turn have a priority of meaning, for they are the values which bestow significance on the lower ones, giving them relative authority in their own right as well as clarifying their import for the realization of higher values. Values at the pole of ultimacy play a decisive role in authorizing the full range of values present in human experience. They ground the totality of the value realm. They also provide the determinative criteria for ranking the various modalities of value appearing to consciousness. It is in this sense that they are ultimate.[36]

There are important cultural variations in the manner in which these different modalities of value are interpreted and explicated. Yet there are solid grounds for arguing that the fundamental structures underlying them and their relations with one another transcend our concrete experiences and perceptions of value and also the multiple cultural forms which express the explicit value ideals of diverse human communities. In these respects their claims to a status of a priority are deserving of thoughtful consideration.

Summary and Conclusion

I have been tracing the manner in which the latent valuation ingredient in human deciding and acting becomes explicit and hence available to self-conscious and critical value judgments. I have argued that this explicitness is achieved by reducing to their value essences the concrete goods encountered in actions aimed at meeting human needs. It is the appearance of these value essences, made possible through the revelatory power of positive affective experiences, which establishes these concrete goods as goods. This effort to bring to light specific value essences also entails seeking a priori grounds for the ranking of values. I stressed the promise of Ricoeur's polar image of value relations, where distinctively social values mediate between the finitude of vital values and the infinitude of values bearing the weight of ultimacy. Making values and their relations fully explicit completes the account of the relation of values to the fulfillment of human needs.

CONCLUDING OBSERVATIONS

It is now possible to restate the basic thesis of this paper. Values appear, I have been claiming, *in* the motivation of specific projects and *by means of* needs which the projects aim to meet. This formulation highlights the essential connections values have to the gratification of needs, needs which reflect the belonging of consciousness to body, to a natural environment, to other selves, to communities, to Being itself. Yet values cannot be simply equated with those objects, processes, and relations which satisfy human needs. They are a priori with respect both to those needs and the means of their gratification—ordering, interpreting, and ranking them even as they bestow significance upon them. If the values which are latent in the motivation of projects are to become fully explicit so as to make possible critical value judgments, then the concrete goods which meet human needs must be reduced to their a priori value essences. While this reduction involves sustained reflective effort—much of which is already displayed in human languages about values—it leads finally to an original recognition of values which is elemental, and hence, is independent of other modalities of meaning. These value essences alone are able to bestow a seal of approval upon the motives functioning to justify our specific projects. Not only is the appearance of values inseparably linked to the gratification of human needs, but, in becoming fully explicit, values also manifest their transcendence over concrete needs. They become forms of meaning which permit us to authorize, rank, and weigh critically the import of our various needs in the total economy of human activity.

What do we gain by portraying the link between values and human needs in this fashion? Two points deserve special emphasis. First, establishing this connection clarifies the relevance for ethics of empirical studies of human needs and their relation to human behavior. Such studies can shed light on what H. Richard Niebuhr calls the "nature and tendency" of beings.[37] In so doing they can provide concrete guidance for our efforts to promote values in human existence, once we have uncovered values which authorize the quest to fulfill human potentialities.

Yet establishing this connection in the manner suggested by Ricoeur's studies permits us at the same time to display the distinctiveness of value judgments, their autonomy with respect to our practical efforts to get what we think we need. We gain a warrant for developing a systematic value theory in genuine independence of the understandings of behavior offered in the human sciences.

Second, clarifying the connection between human needs and values permits us to overcome the false opposition between egoism and altruism in moral discourse. On the one hand, pure egoism, when consistently pursued, emerges as a self-defeating stance. The fulfillment of our needs itself gains significance only with reference to values which transcend those needs even as they are concretely embodied in the means of need-gratification. In discovering the value of other persons and of the power of Being itself, we see the necessity of a relative decentering of our egoistic orientation to life in the interest of our ego-fulfillment. On the other hand, a purely altruistic understanding of the moral life is equally precluded. Our promotion of values worthy of sustained allegiance embraces the possibility of our own fulfillment as persons. The value realm, in other words, bears *promise* as its basic meaning even as it calls us to loyalties which draw us out of the narrow confines of our preoccupation with self-protection and self-promotion. To speak theologically, clarifying the need-value relation uncovers the preeminance of grace over command at primordial levels of pre-reflective experience. We thus gain a kind of phenomenological confirmation of the most profound dialectic of the Christian message: "The one who seeks to save his [or her] life will lose it; but the one who loses his [or her] life for my [Jesus'] sake and the Gospel's will find it."

NOTES

1. H. Richard Niebuhr, "The Center of Value," in *Radical Monotheism and Western Culture* (New York: Harper & Row, 1943), 103.

2. Kant, *Fundamental Principles of the Metaphysics of Morals*, 71.

3. Even Kant, having once sharply separated the principle of morality from any concern for happiness, returns to treat the desire for happiness as an essential ingredient in the "highest good." Unfortunately, the connection Kant establishes between morality and happiness is finally ex-

termal and even arbitrary in light of the prior insistence upon their radical difference. I believe that the distinction and relation of morality and human fulfillment can be more adequately formulated. Cf. Immanuel Kant, *Critique of Practical Reason*, Eng. trans. Lewis White Beck (New York: The Library of Liberal Arts, 1956), 128–36.

4. The following discussion draws heavily upon Paul Ricoeur, *Philosophie de la Volonté: Le Volontaire et L'Involontaire* (Paris: Éditions Montaigne, 1950). Eng. trans. Erazim V. Kohák, *Freedom and Nature*. Subsequent references will be to the original French.

5. Ricoeur, *Le Volontaire et L'Involontaire*, 72.

6. Ibid., 82.

7. Needs, too, have *un contour*, Ricoeur notes, in contrast to *une forme*; so they must not be understood as without structure. Cf. ibid., 86. The form which interests Ricoeur is linked to the function of motivating a project. It is the active forming of needs in the context of deciding and acting that he wishes to stress. The English translation obscures this point.

8. Ricoeur, *Le Volontaire et L'Involontaire*, 85.

9. Ibid., 92.

10. The role of culture and society in regulating the gratification of human needs, even at the organic level, itself testifies to the availability of human needs to the will, sharply distinguishing need patterns from the relative completeness and autonomy of animal instincts.

11. Ricoeur, *Le Volontaire et L'Involontaire*, 90.

12. Ibid.

13. Note Max Scheler's important distinction between goods and values, which Ricoeur seems to presuppose. Cf. Max Scheler, *Formalism in Ethics and Non-Formal Ethics of Values*, Eng. trans. Manfred S. Frings and Roger L. Funk (Evanston, Ill.: Northwestern University Press, 1973), 19–23.

14. Ricoeur, *Le Volontaire et L'Involontaire*, 117.

15. Ibid., 122.

16. This theme is treated in chap. 2 of this volume, "Hospitality to the Stranger."

17. Ricoeur, *Le Volontaire et L'Involontaire*, 452.

18. Paul Ricoeur, *Philosophie de la Volonté: Finitude et Culpabilité*, vol. 1: *L'Homme Fallible* (Paris: Aubier, Éditions Montaigne, 1960), 97–148. Eng. trans. Charles Kelbley, *Fallible Man* (Chicago: Henry Regnery, 1965). Subsequent references will be to the original French.

19. Paul Ricoeur, *The Symbolism of Evil*, Eng. trans. Emerson Buchanan (Boston: Beacon Press, 1969), 232–78, 306–46.

20. Paul Ricoeur, *Freud and Philosophy: An Essay on Interpretation*, Eng. trans. Denis Savage (New Haven and London: Yale University Press, 1970), 528. Cf. also "Paul Ricoeur on Biblical Hermeneutics," *Semeia* 4 (Missoula, Mont.: Scholars Press, 1975), 138.

21. This three-fold scheme by no means makes explicit the full range of value types which might be identified and singled out. By way of comparison, Max Scheler differentiates a stratum of sensible values—the agreeable and the disagreeable—in contrast to organic values. Organic values are associated with general feelings of vitality and well-being as opposed to the immediacy of positive and negative sensations. Scheler names the "historical level" the realm of spiritual values. Within spiritual values he distinguishes aesthetic, moral, and cognitive values. Moral values concern an "objective order of right" [Rechtsordnung] which founds the possibilities of a "life-community" and of the state, and within the latter, of a system of positive law. Moral values, thus, are associated with social institutions, or better, with their valuative foundations. To these sub-types, Scheler might have added technical values. On this latter point, cf. Tillich, *Systematic Theology* 3: 57–62, 258–60. Here technique gets independent treatment as an expression of human cultural creativity. Scheler treats the values which I have associated with Ricoeur's account of consent as values of the holy. The relevant feeling states range, Scheler suggests, from "blissfulness" to "despair." He suggests an intimate connection between the apprehension of the holy and the recognition of the value of the person, including personal community. The decisive point of contact with the ultimate, he is implying, is not experience of limitation such as Ricoeur recounts in his discussion of necessity: temperament, the unconscious, birth and death. It is rather the encounter with the personal "other" as inviolable limit. This theme has gained classic expression in Martin Buber's *I and Thou*, Eng. trans. Ronald Gregor Smith (New York: Charles Scribner's Sons, 1958), especially Part 3, pp. 73–120. It is elaborated in Immanuel Levinas's thought, especially *Totality and Infinity*, 214, 246, 291, 293, et al. For my discussion of Levinas, see chap. 2, "Hospitality to the Stranger." Not only does the personal other mediate the holy; it is through the other, his or her love, that I receive my own worth as a person. And ultimately this self-worth too stems from the holy. It is salvation. Thus, the power and validity of spiritual values, including moral values, are grounded in values of the holy. Scheler summarizes these themes in *Formalism in Ethics and Non-Formal Ethics of Values*, 105–10. Chap. 6, pp. 370–595, provides an extended discussion of the value of the person and of personal community.

Other ways of organizing values are also possible, and likely to be quite illuminating, depending upon one's purposes. Culture, as well as the specific interests motivating one's inquiries, plays a major role in the formulation of such schemes.

22. Cf., e.g., Ricoeur's *Interpretation Theory*, 20–21.

23. Ricoeur, *L'Homme Fallible*, 101.

24. Ibid.

25. Ibid., 104.

26. Cf., e.g., Husserl, *The Crisis of European Sciences and Transcendental Phenomenology*, 149.

27. Ricoeur, *L'Homme Fallible*, 106.

28. Cf. ibid., where Ricoeur speaks of an *a priori* preferential order as intrinsic to the meaning of value.

29. Ricoeur, *Le Volontaire et L'Involontaire*, 116. In his discussion of organic values Ricoeur resists the idea of a pre-given value hierarchy. He stresses instead the heterogeneity of organic values. It is only as they become motives for possible projects that these values gain a common denominator. Cf. ibid., 115–16. His point is well taken when the theme is concrete decision making. As I will emphasize later, recognition of a general pattern of value relations does not in itself tell us what to do in a particular situation. I cannot, however, see how Ricoeur might sustain his claim that the organic values he actually treats—assimilative values, security, exercise, and rest—are as heterogenous as he indicates. They certainly are not a buzzing confusion. All rather clearly function in diverse ways in organic well-being. So even though we may actualize them in various ways and not give them the same importance in our lives, we unavoidably attend to all of them in some balanced fashion as a condition of our existence.

30. Ricoeur, *L'Homme Fallible*, 107–22.

31. Ibid., 122–42. Ricoeur designates the three principal passions as *pouvoir, avoir* and *valoir*. Guided by the thought of Reinhold Niebuhr and Paul Tillich, I have myself attempted to set forth the positive and negative valences of power. See my "Power and Human Fulfillment," *Pastoral Psychology* 22/216 (September 1971): 42–53.

32. Cf. Scheler on the notion of personal community, *Formalism in Ethics and Non-Formal Ethics of Values*, 526–61. Scheler distinguishes personal community from a mass, from life-communities (natural, highly homogenous communities where the individual person has not yet emerged as a distinctive bearer of value), from societies (contractually based societies of essentially self-interested individuals), and from collective societies (based on an assumption of shared interests). In personal communities, persons are differentiated as unique centers of meaning and value, but in a fashion that preserves their mutual belonging to one another. The church is for Scheler the prototype of the latter.

33. Ricoeur discusses and defends his terminology in *L'Homme Fallible*, 22–24.

34. Ricoeur frequently orients his various studies of value and of language to the contributions of reflective philosophy. In particular he takes as central Jean Nabert's account of the human struggle and desire to exist. Cf., e.g., *Freud and Philosophy*, 42–47. In *L'Homme Fallible*, which is dedicated to the memory of Jean Nabert, this struggle and desire to exist is treated as the meaning of the ethical, understood in

the most comprehensive sense. The theme of the book is "the grandeur and limits of an ethical vision of the world." The grandeur of such a vision stems from the attempt to grasp the human struggle and desire to exist under the category of freedom. Its limit reflects the profound reality of evil, which continually distorts that struggle and desire. Nabert's importance for Ricoeur is manifest in his attention to these two motifs in their relationship. See *L'Homme Fallible*, 15. Nabert's most important treatment of this theme is found in his *Elements for an Ethic*. Cf. also Jean Nabert, *Le Désir de Dieu* (Paris: Aubier, 1966).

35. Scheler, e.g., organizes value clusters as strata. Cf. *Formalism in Ethics and Non-Formal Ethics of Values*, 105–10. In this context one might recall Tillich's preference for the term "dimensions" over "levels" in discussing the distinctions and relations among the various "life" realms. Life in Tillich's usage is, of course, a metaphysical category, the most encompassing term for characterizing the nature of being. Dimensions, Tillich suggests, can interpenetrate one another, whereas levels cannot. Cf. *Systematic Theology* 3: 15. Tillich identifies four dimensions, which might be compared with the three value clusters emphasized by Ricoeur: the inorganic, the organic, the psychic, and the spiritual. Ibid., 18–25. The psychic dimension is fairly restricted in its significance, referring to consciousness only. The spiritual dimension embraces the values disclosed by the passions as well as their ultimate reference in the holy.

36. Cf. H. Richard Niebuhr, "The Center of Value," 109.

37. H. Richard Niebuhr, "The Center of Value," 103.

4

THE ACTIVITY OF INTERPRETING IN MORAL JUDGMENT

Twentieth century work in Christian ethics is, by and large, marked by a strong historical consciousness. Most students in the field would readily concede, for example, that any normative understandings they might be able to attain in their constructive thinking will reflect in significant measure their concrete social and cultural locations. We no longer seek the absolute and the final; we search instead for the pertinent and the timely. Nonetheless, we do not so easily incorporate the awareness of our historicity into our deliberations in a material fashion. More often that awareness functions as little more than a formal footnote on what we do, a general acknowledgment that our thinking is, after all, historically conditioned. All the while, our actual procedures of inquiry and patterns of reasoning move in directions which are scarcely historical in their basic thrust.

For recent Christian ethics in America, the analysis and constructive development of the logic of moral discourse has in particular enjoyed widespread appeal.[1] For this style of reasoning, the crucial test of a moral notion is likely to be a version of the Kantian insistence on universalizable principles, e.g., a principle of "informed consent," or of "equality of opportunity," or more broadly, that "like cases be treated alike." There is much to be said for reasoning that reaches toward principles of this sort. It gives a public form to moral judgments. It permits, even requires, rigorous arguments in support of those judgments. When it is appropriately carried out, it leads to a clarification and adjudication of many troublesome human conflicts. Not less important, it enables us to resist a reduction of our primary moral intuitions to mere subjective preferences or to contingent functions of mechanisms of socialization.

Even so, it is my contention that the heavy emphasis on universalizable principles as the privileged means of determining the content of our moral obligations needs to be qualified by a more substantive historical sensibility. Though principles of this kind enjoy formal clarity and precision, they always carry with them unstated and even unacknowledged meanings and assumptions of a more concrete sort. The accompanying meanings and assumptions tend, moreover, to affect decisively the specific applications of the principles themselves. When moral principles are applied without critical awareness of the concrete meanings associated with them, they are apt in their universalistic grandeur to serve as ideological cover for what is actually going on.

Current attempts to promote equality of opportunity by means of "affirmative action" provide a case in point. In seeking to implement affirmative action concretely, we are likely to discover that the qualifications governing access to various positions and opportunities contain largely unexamined cultural, racial, and sexual biases which are not manifestly relevant to the tasks in view. If we cannot correct these biases, the equality we champion will turn out to be merely formal. In terms of actual, material results, life chances will continue to be heavily weighted in favor of some at the expense of others. Justice cannot be served in this situation by straightforward appeals to the basic moral principle alone. We also require means of exposing the biases present in the application of the principle, and of negotiating a new understanding of its import for the concrete realities we face.[2]

The point is not wholly to deny the moral significance of universalizable principles. It is to qualify substantially our use of them. We simply are not able in practice to think about concrete moral problems in strictly universal terms. In making such an attempt, we invariably have in mind certain more specific associations—for example, concerning proper behavior, respectively, for women and men. We cannot make suitable use of the principles if we cannot at the same time attend critically to the associations.

Put more strongly still, our apprehension of the meaning of our basic moral notions is limited and conditioned by "prejudices," conventional understandings which reflect the impact of the past upon our particular orientations to worldly realities.[3] These prejudices normally conceal from view the social and cultural specificity of the notions we hold, and perhaps also their more radical implications for human social existence. A predominantly historical mode of thought, I am suggesting, would alert us to the presence and operation of these prejudices. For such thinking, we cannot respond to concrete situations simply by unfolding the logic of our basic moral convictions and then applying the results in specific policies and actions. We must rather give considerable attention to interpreting the readings of those situations which are held by actors—especially representative actors—who are more or less directly involved in them. Moral reasoning, we could say, requires a hermeneutic, an approach to elucidating the meaning of what is going on which permits us to check the prejudices shaping our ways of being in the world against the understandings of those differently situated.

Carrying out this kind of inquiry involves some fundamental shifts in our standard ways of thinking about ethics. And these shifts present some difficult methodological problems, especially if they are to be accomplished in a rigorously critical way.

The present study is largely methodological. It is concerned with establishing a conceptual framework within which we might take up the hermeneutical aspects of ethical inquiry. I shall argue that Edmund Husserl's notion of the life-world, especially its primacy vis-à-vis the abstractions of the sciences, permits us to specify the frame of reference within which an ethical hermeneutic finds its proper home.

This undertaking builds directly on Gibson Winter's characterization of ethics as "an evaluative hermeneutics of history."[4] Winter himself uses the notion of the life-world in working out the relation in policy studies between ethical discourse and the human sciences. However, I likewise see a phenomenology of the life-world and of the hermeneutics to which it gives rise as offering the most promising way to carry out H. Richard Niebuhr's proposal for an "ethics of responsibility."[5] Broadly speaking, I am seeking to contribute to the style of thinking which Niebuhr and Winter have in common.

MODELS OF INTERPRETING
AND THEIR RELATION TO
ETHICAL REFLECTION

For an ethics of the fitting, H. Richard Niebuhr contends, the prior question is this: "What is going on?"[6] Only in light of a more or less satisfactory answer to this question can we take up appropriately the matter of a fitting response. The important thing to note is that the apprehension of the meaning and significance of a situation is itself already a moral task, not a mere recounting of facts which is only preliminary to moral and ethical reflection proper.[7] Such interpretation is a moral undertaking in at least three respects. First, careful attention to what is going on is itself a moral obligation. We cannot immediately assume that we know the meaning of what we observe. We must open ourselves to instruction by those who are involved in or likely to be affected by what we observe.

Second, relevant normative considerations are already ingredient in the unfolding situation we are seeking to interpret. We do not need, at least not in the first instance, to introduce such considerations from elsewhere. These considerations themselves offer suggestions about the fitting, and hence, make claims upon our potentialities as actors. Discerning how they present themselves in concrete situations and with what force is then a feature in recounting what is going on.

Finally, our re-presentation of the normative meanings present in a situation itself contributes substantively to our determination of the fitting. For many typical cases, of course, a correct reading of what is going on effectively indicates the fitting response. That is, if the situation we are seeking to understand turns out to correspond in all relevant respects to cases whose moral meaning we have already resolved in previous deliberations, then having recognized the correspondence, we know what to do—at least until further notice. I add this last phrase as a reminder that even the most typical cases contain latent meanings which, if fully appreciated and explicated, might lead us to change our views. However, many situations, especially in the broader social world, call for a work of the imagination, perhaps even riskful experimentation, if we are to approximate something akin to a "fitting" response. Venturing the fitting then involves a creative transformation of the possibilities present in the situation, the generation of a "new order of the world." Even in these instances we cannot in our creativity simply leap over existing moral realities. We must in some fashion come to grips with what is already given if our actions are to be relevant and effective.

The genius of Niebuhr and Winter, I would suggest, is that they locate the burden of ethical understanding and of concrete moral choice in the historically formed situations of social interaction among human beings, and in the matrix of socially shared meanings which order those interactions.

Here we come to the central methodological problem: How are we to understand the question "what is going on?" as itself a moral question, especially since the dominant models for narrating and analyzing events seek to limit and control for evaluative judgments of this sort? We can grasp the force of this question by bringing into view two basic approaches to the "reading" of situations. Both are relevant to ethical understanding, yet neither can as such assist us in discerning the moral meanings which are formative of those situations.

The first of these is the ideal of the newspaper reporter or of a witness at a jury trial. The standard is to recount with the highest possible accuracy just the "facts," what can be seen and heard in a course of events, including reports of what others actually said and did with regard to those events. Here one must resist the temptation to draw conclusions or to offer evaluative judgments, even when they seem fairly obvious. It must be left to others to venture such judgments. For this model of reporting, one presents selected features of a situation, ideally the most pertinent ones, in their purest contingency as factual givens. The underlying presumption would seem to be that these features of experience are the decisive constituents of reality, or at least of what we can call "objective" reality. Other sorts of considerations, especially value judgments and feeling-level responses, are founded on this primary stratum of empirical fact. In relation to its manifest objectivity, they are more subjective in their cognitive status.[8]

In order to limit the sheer contingency of the facts gathered through empirical observations, the work of reporting may be extended by giving it a historical turn. Then one narrates the longer or shorter sequences of events in the lives of the relevant actors, including their typical patterns of interaction, in order to see whether significant regularities can be discerned. These regularities give a certain order, a certain shape to our expectations, even though their contingent status is still not essentially altered.

A second basic approach to the reading of situations is more characteristic of the human sciences. This approach does not content itself with simply reporting facts as contingently given. It ventures conclusions of a specific sort about those facts. In particular it seeks to isolate certain underlying factors, typically present in human activity, whose operation permits us to see the "necessities" that condition and control seemingly contingent happenings.[9] To get at these factors we require theory, theory which permits us to see the facts in a new way and to make in our interpretive activity a more pertinent selection among the facts which do appear. The function of the theory is to enable us to "explain" happenings with reference to certain dynamics at work in them. Value orientations of various sorts are, of course, among the phenomena which psychologists and social scientists seek to study, but precisely as regulative features of human experience, not as challenges to creative and transforming responses to particular types of situations. Various human sciences, to be sure, have value biases of their own, as many critics have shown.[10] These biases lead to "explanations" which carry strong normative suggestions about action and social policy. If, however, the biases themselves—which are often unintended or perhaps operationally unavoidable—are to be evaluated, a shift in method is necessary, one which takes us outside of the reach of the empirical sciences as such.

Insofar as human science perspectives can enable us to surface the conditioning factors which both limit and render possible various kinds of concrete developments, so the same perspectives can also shed light on the longer or shorter sequences of happenings which are of interest to the historian. In this case the methods and the theoretical perspectives of the human sciences are themselves put in the service of historical understanding.

Thus, we have two basic approaches to "what is going on": the accurate recounting of empirical facts in their contingent givenness, and the theoretical uncovering of the underlying regularities which permit us to "explain" those facts as having a certain "necessity." For convenience, I shall refer to the former as "empirical descriptions" and the latter as "scientific explanations." This analytic summary of contemporary forms of inquiry provides the context for my principal point: if we are to take up the question "what is going on?" as a *moral* question, then neither empirical descriptions nor scientific explanations can, despite their relevance to our inquiry, provide adequate guidance for our work. In fact, if these approaches and their various modifications are fully adequate for setting forth the realities we face in our world, then the interpretation of events cannot in itself be a form of moral inquiry.

It is, of course, quite possible to establish the autonomy and significance of moral and ethical inquiry without challenging the authority of empirical descriptions and scientific explanations for providing us with the most objective accounts of what is going on. For one thing, we can proceed on the assumption that moral (and religious) interpretations of events are essentially subjective, at least when compared with more empirical ways of proceeding. Moral "readings," for this response, do not tell us so much about what is actually going on as about the beliefs and convictions of the interpreter. More elementally, they articulate a particular actor's dispositions and attitudes toward what is taking place. Interpretations of this sort are able to touch the wellsprings of motivation; they also thematize the general intentions appropriate for those sharing a given evaluative orientation to reality. Yet if these subjective beliefs and attitudes are to be brought into relation with worldly realities, they must, for this view, be rendered congruent with empirical descriptions and scientific explanations of the situations in question.

James Gustafson's approach to the interpretation of situations basically fits this pattern, especially when he is seeking to relate theological understandings to particular problems.[11] Indeed, he also reads H. Richard Niebuhr in the same fashion, e.g., in his discussion of Niebuhr's interpretation of World War II as "crucifixion."[12] Gustafson notes, to be sure, that theologians who have had great confidence in the heuristic power of Christian symbols and concepts for illuminating historical events have either consciously stated or quietly assumed that their use is the only way to grasp what is "really" happening.[13] Yet when he elaborates what is "heuristic" about such notions, he returns to accounts of the beliefs and convictions, the dispositions and attitudes, of moral actors.[14] In a strict sense, moreover, these subjective aspects of the self are treated either as matters of more or less arbitrary personal choice or as indications of the ways in which we have been socialized. Gustafson does not take up the question of how these beliefs and convictions might facilitate a truer "seeing" of what is going on, and hence, a more adequate reading of events.[15] Still less does he consider the possibility that moral and religious understandings might themselves be "disclosive" of what is happening.

This subjective response is by no means wholly off the mark. It heightens our awareness of the fact that values can appear to us as significant, meaningful, and authoritative only insofar as they already call forth our commitment. Values are self-involving by their very nature. Using phenomenological language, commitment and conviction designate the modalities of consciousness which correspond to the appearance of value-type meanings.[16] This response also leads quite naturally to a more systematic consideration of moral agency, especially those habitualities and continuities in the self which give stability and depth to action. But from the standpoint of phenomenological understandings, Gustafson's treatment of the subjective quality of our beliefs, attitudes, and intentions is abstract, that is, isolated from the concreteness of our worldly being. This abstractness would appear to be the inevitable counterpart of his prior failure to appreciate the abstractness of empirical descriptions and scientific explanations as procedures for grasping what is going on.

There is a second way of establishing the autonomy and distinctiveness of moral inquiry while yet conceding to empirical description and scientific explanation complete sovereignty for getting at "what is going on." In contrast to the realm of fact, of what *is* the case, one can identify a realm of ought, or of values, as the proper province of moral and ethical inquiry. The student of ethics then seeks to clarify the sort of objectivity and the methods of its realization that are appropriate to this latter realm. The most effective response of this type in Anglo-American thought has an analytical-logical form.[17] I shall for convenience refer to it, therefore, as the analytical-logical approach. The distinctive business of ethics in this frame of reference is not the description of events, but the identification and clarification of the values which lay claim to our loyalties, or the formulation of the principles and rules which ought to govern our actions.

Analytical-logical approaches to ethics continue, of course, to be interested in matters of fact and in scientific accounts of the "laws" which explain connections among facts. For such approaches, we are interested in matters of fact in part because we want to know what sorts of actions are realistically possible in a situation. We also want to know, to the degree that we are able, the probable outcomes of particular interventions in that situation. From the standpoint of what is distinctive about ethics, however, our interest in the facts of a case is chiefly to determine the appropriate classification of the morally significant features of a situation. In identifying permissible forms of experimentation on human subjects, we want to know whether a fetus scheduled for abortion is, in the relevant respects, essentially like a terminally ill patient or perhaps a condemned prisoner, or whether it is more akin to an unwanted growth about to be removed through a surgical procedure.[18] Similarly, in assessing possible foreign policy initiatives, we want to know whether a given instance of civil strife, especially one in which external assistance is being given to rebel bands, fits our criteria of "just" counter-insurgency warfare, or whether it is more a case of "just" revolution.[19] Once we identify the type of case exemplified by a particular situation, we will know what value considerations have normative weight or what moral principles and rules apply. Novel situations will, to be sure, continually arise which present us with new problems for ethical analysis, such as the recent advances in biomedical sciences or the emerging evidence of the "limits to growth" on planet earth. But the proper business of specialists in ethics nonetheless centers in the realm of the ought or of the desirable, not in the realm of fact, though the realm of fact must, of course, be subject in principle to penetration and alteration by means of transcendent ethical possibilities.[20] Here too, religious convictions would seem to enter into play chiefly as motivators to action of the right sort, and as ultimate warrants for taking moral obligations seriously or for honoring and serving certain fundamental values. For some thinkers, e.g., Paul Ramsey, they may provide the essential content of the moral life as well, though that content may also be presumed to make positive contact with the understandings of morally serious persons who do not share the same religious commitments.

In neither of the two approaches I have sketched, the subjectivist or the analytical-logical, can it be said, with H. Richard Niebuhr, that the prior question for the moral actor is "what is going on?" In the first response, the prior question would appear to be this: "How do Christian convictions form lives?"[21] In the latter, it is more apt to be this: "What principles and rules ought to govern human actions in various types of situations?" Or, "What values are worthy of our loyalty in human affairs, and how are they to be ordered when they are in apparent conflict?" In what frame of reference, then, are we to place Niebuhr's question? My claim, as I noted earlier, is that this frame of reference can be uncovered by phenomenological studies of the life-world and by the hermeneutics to which they give rise.

THE STRUCTURES OF THE LIFE-WORLD AS THE MATRIX FOR INTERPRETING

Edmund Husserl's most important achievement was his discovery of the primacy of the life-world.[22] His central interest was not in ethics, though he did believe that his studies had important ethical implications.[23] It was rather in the sciences, more specifically in establishing an epistemological foundation for the sciences. His quest eventually led him to the life-world, the world of lived experience, as the source and basis of the sciences—of their underlying assumptions and warrants, of their methodologies, of their basic concepts. His specific task was to undertake a science of the life-world itself, i.e., a systematic articulation of its constitutive features, pursued to the point of making explicit their apodictic self-evidence. Yet by establishing the primacy of the life-world, he incidentally served ethical understanding, delineating a frame of reference within which the concrete, historically situated character of moral discourse might be grasped and elaborated.[24]

What is meant by the life-world? It is not possible to re-present in a concrete description the full richness and density of the life-world itself. What I shall offer is a general characterization aimed at orienting our thinking. The characterization is ordered in terms of four categories which have become central in phenomenological investigations: intentionality (especially its articulation in the Heideggerian notion of being-in-the-world),[25] intersubjectivity, temporality, and embodiment. These categories have emerged as central in phenomenology by virtue of their constitutive role in our apprehension of those meanings which make up our pre-reflective lived experience.

To begin with, the life-world appears to consciousness at its most primordial level as already meaningful, and meaningful precisely in terms of our concern-filled engagements with it. "World" does not first appear as aggregations of sense data requiring synthesis through some sort of associative processes (e.g., David Hume), still less as raw material calling forth theoretical inquiries into its underlying regularities. It comes as primordially ordered, and ordered with respect to our existential involvements. It is world for *my* being: as threatening, but also as serviceable, indeed, as essential to my survival and flourishing; as familiar, as suffused with cumulative memories of affectively rich experiences, but also as strange, even disconcerting in its presentation of novelties; as a barrier to my projects, as frustration to my longings, desires, even my most pressing needs, but more fundamentally, as an open field for the articulation of my distinctive possibilities. We can, with Husserl, speak of world in terms of intentionality, as consisting in the presentation of various modalities of sense to corresponding acts of consciousness. Yet as life-world, these forms of sense bear most essentially on our struggles to exist and to discover value in our existing. Thus, in disclosing itself to us as world of our concern-filled engagements, it also discloses our being as belonging to the world, as being-in-the-world.

The life-world is a social world. It is intersubjectively constituted. It consists centrally in shared meanings awakened and mediated through our interactions with others: predecessors and contemporaries, even successors; associates with whom we enter into face-to-face contact and anonymous others who impact our lives only indirectly.[26] In fact, the world can have the sense "objective world" only because of the pre-given possibilities of intersubjectively shared perspectives on the world, of what Husserl called the "reciprocity of perspectives."[27] The "others" who appear to me as beings like myself present to me, on the one hand, the primal opportunities of my being: identity as an individual self, feelings of self-worth, the summons to responsibility, the solicitation to charity, a sense of the meaningfulness of existence which enables me to accept and embrace my finitude, my inescapable vulnerability and frailty, even my sin. In general we can say that the particular meanings which bear to us the concrete sense of world and of its valuation are generated, sustained, mediated, and reinforced in the interactions which form the social world. World is in fundamental respects a "social construction." But the "others" who offer me life and worth are, on the other hand, and precisely by virtue of their power to bestow life, also the most serious threats to my being, more serious than the most overpowering terrors of the "natural" world. They lure me into mindless conventionality and dull my uneasy conscience; they shake my self-esteem with their judgmental attitudes, or by simply passing me by as nonentity. And for many, all too many, certain "others" reveal themselves as oppressors, persecutors, exploiters, as sources of violence, cruelty, interminable suffering. Whatever the specific modalities of human interaction, however, the life-world is always a social world. And prior to all empirical studies of the operations of human societies, prior to all sociological theories aimed at explaining those operations, the social world is already ingredient in our pre-reflective, lived experience. It is a feature in our practical, everyday dealings with others who enter directly or indirectly into those meanings which make up our sense of world.

The life-world is temporal. In each interaction and in each worldly engagement we live out of the past toward an open future. Our way of being in every present is structured by the simultaneous interpenetration of past and future. Our memories—individual and collective, conscious and unconscious—give substance to our being, bestow upon us our identities, order and orient our expectations. In so doing, they transmit to us the power to act in determinate ways in concert with our fellow human beings. Our anticipations, on the other hand, stretch out toward an open horizon before which we can reorder and reorient our ways of being in the world, projecting ourselves on the world in a manner in keeping with our fundamental potentialities-for-being. Yet temporal experience also has its profound ambiguities. The past which offers us identity and substance also restricts and limits us. It burdens us with disappointments, frustrations, rejections, injuries at the hands of others; it weighs us down with guilty recollections of our own deceit, timidity, self-protectiveness, cruelty. In its negative face it mocks our presumed powers of acting, somberly reminding us that there is nothing new under the sun. Likewise, the open possibilities which offer the promise of renewal, opportunities for fresh starts, also bring threats of loss, of disintegrative social change, of failure, of the collapse of meaning, and finally of aging, death, and nothingness. Beneath and prior to all of our rational procedures for organizing the uses of time or for reckoning temporal sequences is the pre-reflective experience of temporality as a constituent in the ambiguities of the life-world.[28]

Finally, the life-world is ordered with reference to our being as body, and affectively colored by means of its sensibilities. Body marks my location in the world, as though, Schutz suggests, I were the zero point between two coordinates which delineate the reaches of the world.[29] It is always with reference to this zero point that the world and its realities are spatially distributed, as either near or far, as within my reach or within my attainable reach, or as beyond my reach. Body is also the medium for my apprehension of the world's significations, which means not simply that my sense organs receive sense data, but also that my affective responses, not readily localizable, disclose to me the valuation of the world, or perhaps more accurately, my belonging to the world. Finally, body is my "instrument," my "vehicle," for acting in and on the world. It is my possibility for moving about in the world and for manipulating the materials of the world in terms of my purposes, for relating to others and communicating with them in word, gesture, touch.[30] Yet body as lived, my body and your body, reflects some of the same sorts of ambiguities which we have noted with reference to other structures of the life-world. Body which offers me the capacity to move about, the resources to manipulate the materials of my environment, and the means of communicating with others is also body which fails me through injury, disease, advancing age, and death. Body which is the medium of pleasure, of positive affective experiences, is at the same time the possibility for excruciating pain, pain which overwhelms me and destroys my sense of self. Even its promises of pleasure are problematic, for they tempt me to violate commitments, to distort priorities and flee responsibilities. And while body situates me spatially, it also isolates me, marking out a dimension of experiencing which is uniquely my own, which can be shared by no one else. The main point, how-

ever, is that prior to all sorts of physiological or anatomical inquiries, prior to all technical manipulations—say, in medical
practice—the body is always already present to me pre-reflectively as lived body.

As I have indicated, Husserl's interest in taking up the question
of the life-world was to establish its primacy vis-à-vis the abstractions of the sciences. Rather than being highly subjective
modifications of the empirical data—the "hard" data—which
make up the subject matter of the sciences, its constitutive meanings *found* the possibility of scientific inquiry itself. As Alfred
Schutz put it so pointedly: the everyday life world is the "paramount reality."[31] Science emerges as a possible task on the basis
of meanings already present in another form within the life-
world. Science is itself an outgrowth of our concern-filled engagements with the world. On the one hand, it helps us render
intelligible the recalcitrance of the world and our bodies, their
characteristic ways of resisting our projects. On the other hand,
it instructs our expectations of future probabilities by uncovering
the "law-abiding" dynamics which limit and condition the open
possibilities of the world, thus increasing our measure of control
and in the process heightening our answerability for the course
of the world's developments. Yet however impressive the find-
ings of the sciences may be, they cannot displace the life-world
and its distinctive meanings, nor can they shake its primacy. The
scientist may suspend attention to the life-world in her theoriz-
ing, but insofar as she acts upon her world, e.g., in handling
experimental apparatus, or insofar as she interacts with fellow
scientists in her social world, e.g., in working as part of a team
or in communicating the results of her research, she is once again
fully engaged in the life-world. And that engagement becomes
all the more encompassing when at the end of a day's work she
returns to her home and attends to the ordinary tasks of daily
living.

In relation to the life-world, empirical descriptions and scientific explanations are abstract. Indeed, so are ethical theories
and the reasoning they make possible, including theories about
how our subjectively held beliefs and our basic attitudes shape
our typical responses to events. Abstraction is, of course, by no
means a bad thing, provided we keep clearly in view the manner
of its operation in our thinking. In fact, all thought, so far as I

can see, is abstract in one way or another, and the relatively more abstract categories have the merit of being able to unify a broader range of seemingly disparate phenomena. They call attention to similarities among discrete realities, even when they are not obvious. Yet abstractions are finally important not as substitutes for life-world meanings, but as tools to assist us in elucidating their implications and in assessing their import. It is finally in the life-world in its concreteness that we act, and it is action in the life-world that must be served by our analyses and judgments.

This account of the life-world and of its constitutive structures is important because it orients us to the modalities of meaning which are of primary interest in an ethically significant interpretation of "what is going on?" To ask what is going on, or in Winter's terms to undertake an evaluative hermeneutics of history, is to inquire into the concrete meanings which form the life-worlds of the relevant representative actors who are participants in a given situation. Notions of intentionality, intersubjectivity, temporality, and embodiment can guide and organize this inquiry. In this connection, it is noteworthy that both Niebuhr and Winter give specific attention to the first three of these four basic categories in their respective accounts of ethics, though neither has done justice to the notion of embodiment.

For H. Richard Niebuhr these structures appear as constituents of the "responsible life."[32] Responsibility involves response to the actions of others (intersubjectivity) in terms of our interpretation (intentionality) of what is going on (i.e., in the life-world) and in anticipation (temporality) of subsequent responses to our actions by those others (again, intersubjectivity). All of this, he concludes, takes place in an ongoing community of interactions (the life-world as embracing intentionality, intersubjectivity, and temporality). Niebuhr then elaborates his central paradigm with a discussion of sociality and temporality, the latter functioning to show how those meanings which make possible our interpretive activity present themselves to consciousness, both in their givenness and in their open possibilities.[33]

Similarly, Winter's adaptation (with the help of Alfred Schutz) of G. H. Mead's theory of the social constitution of selfhood identifies the intersubjective context in the life-world within which morally significant understandings appear.[34] In Winter's work intentionality does not refer simply to the orientation of consciousness to the presented meanings forming the life-world (Husserl's more precise usage). It also suggests, perhaps more importantly, the active, initiating dynamics of selfhood in contrast to the deterministic tendencies of Mead's thought. It designates my possibilities for taking responsibility for my social world, for reshaping it in terms of its open horizon.[35] The notion of temporality—embracing in unity both the settled past and the open future—permits Winter to relate the freedom of the project (which is of central interest in ethics) to the conditioning and controlling factors that order human action (which are of central interest in the human sciences).[36]

In elaborating his perspective, Winter develops the notion of temporality in terms of the distinctions and relations between what he calls societal identity, cultural integrity, and historical fulfillment. These three categories are associated respectively with past, present, and future in the unity of temporal experience. Thus, he invites us to examine contemporary crises as crises of cultural integrity, and to do so in light of our historical retrieval of the traditions which express our societal identity. These investigations provide the concrete bases upon which we can project future possibilities of social harmony, i.e., reach toward historical fulfillment.[37]

The point of calling attention to the structures which constitute the life-world is to order our reading of its concrete meanings, and to show the senses in which these meanings found the possibilities for the various forms of scientific and ethical abstraction. Put differently, the concrete is not to be equated with empirical data, especially not empirical data cleansed of the rich valuative associations which first draw them to our attention. Still less is the concrete to be equated with scientific theories concerning the underlying regularities in typical sorts of happenings. It concerns the specific meanings which convey to us our sense of world, which situate us in the world in particular ways, which articulate our limits and possibilities as beings-in-the-world. It is to these meanings that an evaluative hermeneutics of history, or an ethics of the fitting, must attend.

THE CONFLICT OF INTERPRETATIONS
Once we have established the frame of reference within which an ethically significant activity of interpreting might take place,

we have by no means solved all of our problems. This framework simply permits us to pose these problems in a more appropriate fashion. To begin with, when we proceed to interpret critically what is going on in a situation, we invariably discover not one, but many meanings, some of which may be widely various, even incompatible. The point is an elementary one. Consider, for example, the range of meanings likely to figure in any concrete assessment of our present ways of organizing and financing the delivery of medical services. How people are situated with reference to the health care system is likely to play a significant role in shaping its manner of appearing to them: the executive of a large insurance company, a salesman for a pharmaceutical firm, a physician specializing in blood diseases, a head nurse on an understaffed hospital floor, a technician who operates complex diagnostic and therapeutic equipment, a middle-class American concerned about the devastating economic consequences of catastrophic illness, a government bureaucrat charged with monitoring medicaid payments, an indigent patient waiting long hours in a crowded clinic at County General for treatment already too long postponed. The concrete meaning-worlds which make up the reality of our health-care system are diverse and conflictual. These meanings, moreover, are scarcely univocal in nature. Any one of them carries with it multiple horizons capable of further elucidation. Thus, the physician who lifts up the sanctity of the physician-patient relationship is likely to activate notions of professional dominance (and status!) and technical rationality along with the more favored images of humanitarian concern, or loyalty to the Hippocratic oath. Examples can be readily multiplied.

For a phenomenological hermeneutic there is nothing surprising or unnerving about this state of affairs. According to Heidegger, for example, no single articulation of meaning can ever, not even in principle, express in its totality our pre-given, pre-reflective understanding of the way in which a particular occurrence or state of affairs opens up our potentiality for being-in-the-world. In every case more is going on than we can say, and we always understand more than we can make explicit. A particular interpretation, therefore, can only set forth in one specific way the totality of what is already understood at a pre-reflective level.[38] This specific way of taking the meaning of our being-in-

113

the-world, moreover, both obscures and at the same time activates possible alternative articulations of meaning not yet uttered. The finitude of the said, Gadamer notes, is always accompanied by the infinity of the unsaid.[39] In Heidegger's language, every interpretation is a determinate "taking as" of our potentiality for being which invites further interpretations, not as though we could ever finally exhaust the possibilities, but as a way of keeping us open to meanings which are virtual but not yet fully explicit in our thinking.[40]

This fluidity of sense is a precondition, it should be noted, of the creative advance in understanding which is a feature in the temporality of experience. If the formative meanings of the life-world had only *one* sense, allowed only *one* correct interpretation, then transformations in those meanings could never occur within the continuity of a traditioning process. Changes in interpretation would simply mean that the older readings had become, from the vantage point of the present, false. Even more serious, persons holding disparate understandings of human possibility could never come to common understandings, that is, without one or both being exposed as simply mistaken. The virtuality of sense contained in all specific interpretations of human being discloses a dynamic in human understanding which permits movement and growth within a fundamental continuity of meaning. While this fluidity of meaning rules out clear and unequivocal readings of situations, with the illusion of moral security which such certainty might give, it brings more fully to light the role of imagination and creativity in establishing, sustaining, and recreating the reciprocity of understanding among persons which makes fitting action possible.

But not only do we confront in our interpretive activity a multiplicity of meanings and also multiple possible readings of each of these meanings; we also confront meanings and interpretations which distort and conceal rather than articulate and disclose what is going on. Heidegger speaks in this connection of the "fancies" and "popular conceptions" which obscure the sense of our potentiality for being.[41] In social ethics we have to be particularly alert to those fancies and popular conceptions which function to legitimate special privilege, or which justify violence, exploitation, and oppression, however grandly universalistic they may appear to be. Though we seek to be open to the meanings which form the life-worlds of representative actors in a situation, we can never take these meanings at face value without further questioning.

The attempt to apprehend what is going on seems now to have become a virtually impossible task. Not only do we confront an overwhelming multiplicity of meanings, each with its multiplicity of possible interpretations; we also are unsettled from the start by our awareness of the pervasiveness of distortion and concealment in human understanding and discourse. It is no wonder that we seek alternatives to historical thinking in our efforts to reduce complexity to manageable terms.

Unfortunately, Niebuhr himself largely overstepped these difficult matters by relating his account of the responsible life all too directly to radical monotheism.[42] In his thought the responsible life finally entails interpreting all actions upon us as actions of God, so that in all our responses we are also responding to the one God beyond the many. Theologically, I have no basic objection to this formulation, except for what appears at times to be its antipathy to trinitarian formulations of monotheism. Its problem is that it does not permit us to distinguish one situation from another, for all situations and all fitting responses are alike in this respect: they involve the one God and they call for loyalty to Being in the beings. Indeed, one fears that Niebuhr considers all actions *ipso facto* fitting insofar as they are carried out in the spirit of monotheistic faith. That is to say, it is monotheistic faith which renders actions fitting, not concrete, historical pertinence.

Basic theological formulations are crucial to an ethics of the fitting. They articulate a meaning horizon which both frees us to attend solicitously to the conflicting meanings and interpretations which make up the course of human events, and also obliges us, radically and unequivocally, to such care. They make explicit the final sanctions and ultimate warrants for the effort to understand and for the struggles toward human community which understanding makes possible. In specifically Christian terms, the Gospel permits and requires "world openness," an openness which can allow things to show themselves as themselves. It permits and requires such openness because it displays the world as already created, judged, and reconciled by God. Insofar as we enter into that Gospel we can deal with the world's distortions without dread or defensiveness and also participate in its possibilities for reconciliation.

Yet the concrete work of interpreting "what is going on" is not in itself taken care of by this larger horizon of meaning. This meaning horizon equips us for and guides us in the work of interpretation. But the work itself is our free responsibility. How does it proceed? We can, I believe, identify four basic types of interpretive activity which in their distinctiveness and interrelations are capable of ordering and simplifying our common task. I shall refer to these as application, suspicion, retrieval, and hospitality.

Initially we work, quite naturally and appropriately, with the "meanings" at hand, the socially shared stock of knowledge, in interpreting what is going on. We may not even be aware at this level that we are "interpreting" since the conventions which make up our stock of knowledge have a certain self-evidence about them. We rather think of ourselves as simply attending to things the way they are or ought to be. Our task is to "apply" the conventions straightforwardly to concrete cases. And when we confront new cases, we seek to assimilate the novel to the familiar, reading the former in terms of their similarities to and differences from the latter. This conventional wisdom may, as Schutz notes, take the form of "recipe" knowledge, specifications of concrete steps to be followed for dealing with this or that sort of situation, but with no explicitly formulated principles of action.[43]

When critical reason operates upon such knowledge, it transforms the recipes into general principles which are universalizable, enabling actors to think for themselves. Such principles express an imperative to fairness, to treat like cases alike. Much ethical reflection of the analytical-logical sort, I would suggest, tends to be a modification toward precision and consistency of socially shared conventions. It finally rests its case upon appeals to the reasonable, i.e., to what is more or less obvious in a culture, but not necessarily with full awareness of the social and cultural conditionedness of such obviousness. Work in the human sciences, it might also be noted, often appears to be value free because the value orientations upon which it rests are likewise elements in the conventional wisdom of the society. These sciences, e.g., functionalist sociology or welfare economics, serve chiefly to confirm conventional values and to further their fuller and more efficient realization. Yet the authority of these moral principles and of these implicit values derives from their rootage in meanings belonging to the life-worlds of particular groups of actors.

While historical thinking relativizes these processes of "application," it does not render them invalid. We must have shared conventions if ordered social life is to be possible. Moreover, we are not likely to be able to question our conventions, nor is such questioning apt to be fruitful, unless we have specific motivations to do so. Finally, even the most radical revolutions in thought and in social organization depend for their viability on the continuation of many habitual ways of thinking and acting. Everything cannot be "up for grabs" at once. So, interpreting what is going on appropriately begins with application, and in many instances, it ends there as well.

Yet, as I have noted, conventions not only enable life; they also distort it and conceal its richer possibilities. To get at what is going on, therefore, we have need of what Paul Ricoeur has called a "hermeneutics of suspicion."[44] In this mode of interpreting one is not content to accept and apply conventional understandings, not even in the form of universalizable principles. The conventions are rather taken as symptoms of deeper, underlying dynamics which normally escape awareness in ordinary, day-to-day activity, but which nonetheless shed more light on what is actually going on than do the conventions themselves. Ricoeur identifies Friedrich Nietzsche, Karl Marx, and Sigmund Freud as the "masters" of suspicion in this sense, though his own studies are largely confined to the thought of Freud. More generally, he grants legitimacy to any work of suspicion which rests upon what he calls a basic human function.[45] So, Freud's work focuses on the dynamics of desire and on the sublimation of desire required by "civilization"; Marx attends to productive activity and its articulation in a class structure; and Nietzsche examines the "will to power" and the resentment toward the strong which it generates in the weak and timid. And there are other analogous lines of inquiry.

For social ethics, ideological criticism of the sort suggested by Marx's thought has special importance. It alerts us to the fact that the dominant ideas of a society in general are especially favorable to the particular interests of the ruling class. Their function is in significant measure to persuade the less favored, even the oppressed and exploited, to see the "necessity" of their condition and to accept that condition as a feature in the "way things are." For a Christian ethic in particular, critical interpretation must attend to the work of suspicion, testing the impact of conventional wisdom—especially when it is given a sophisticated, rational form—upon "outsiders" and members of the under classes, for these who are "least" among our brothers and sisters bear to us the presence of Christ in the world.

The point of a hermeneutics of suspicion is not finally, however, to displace the meanings which form the life-worlds of representative actors in a situation. Even the understandings of an oppressor class are likely to have some broader significance, for notions which are purely illusory or wholly false are not likely to have sufficient authority to legitimate either privilege or exploitation. Deception is more successful when it makes use of half-truths than when it relies upon straightforward lies. The task, therefore, is to cut through the illusions and concealments in order to release the life-giving power latent in the shared understandings which presently distort and conceal human possibilities. It is to uncover the senses in which those meanings can permit things to show themselves as themselves.

Besides, suspicion itself is not possible apart from meanings incongruent with conventional understandings which are given in the life-worlds of certain representative actors. When black Americans, for example, attend not only to the extent to which they are denied participation in the American dream, but also to the arbitrariness of such denial, they find the resources either to insist on the implementation of the dream or perhaps to question the dream itself. So suspicion does not displace the primacy of the life-world. It is rather activated by features in the life-world. Its import is finally measured, moreover, by the openings it provides for the reordering of the life-world. Suspicion leads to a fresh look at possibilities mediated by the meanings which make up the life-world itself.

Interpretation at this point issues in two processes which are dialectically related. Ricoeur characterizes the first as a "hermeneutics of retrieval" or of "recollection."[46] The second, I would suggest, can appropriately be termed a "hermeneutics of hospitality."[47] The relation between these two modalities of interpreting reflects the interaction between self and other, or between "our" group (class, sex, race, nation, religious orientation, "special" interest, etc.) and those "other" groups with whom we must deal, directly or indirectly.

Retrieval involves a new and deeper engagement with the longer traditions underlying the popular conventions which form present awareness. The presumption is that popular conceptions invariably represent a certain truncation of richer traditions, which would result in a diminution of life were the traditions not from time to time recovered and renewed, perhaps even transformed, in relation to new situations. One criticizes the conventions in terms of the deeper traditions upon which they are founded. And if the conventions have become problematic because of changing social conditions, one presumes that the deeper traditions will offer richer resources for creative thinking, for innovation, than the more surface-level conventions. Rather than foreclosing the future, tradition provides the basis upon which an imaginative production of future alternatives becomes possible. Winter and Niebuhr give explicit attention to this activity of retrieval in ethical and theological understanding.[48] Winter mentions in particular our civil and confessional traditions.[49]

Yet retrieval will not suffice in itself because of its inability to do justice to the problems of pluralism in contemporary life. To balance and limit the recollection of our own heritage, we also have need of a hermeneutics of hospitality, a readiness to welcome strange and unfamiliar meanings into our own awareness, perhaps to be shaken by them, but in no case to be left unchanged. These meanings enable us to become aware of limitations in the concrete historicity of our own view of things. We always come to situations with our particular understandings, our prejudices Gadamer calls them, when we begin to interpret.[50] These prejudices both permit and interfere with understanding. But to ask the question "What is going on?" means to be prepared to discover that we do not already know and understand, that we ourselves are in need of instruction about the moral sense of what is taking place. We need the "others" to instruct us about the meaning of our prejudices, of the world horizon which articulates our way of being-in-the-world. We need to give special weight and care to those meaning-worlds which are not normally taken seriously in the social interactions within which we participate from day to day: the understandings of the poor, women, and minorities. These "others" must be taken seriously not simply in a spirit of tolerance but in the interest of uncovering the truth. As G. F. W. Hegel pointed out, the "slave" knows two worlds, his own and the one his master imposes on him, while the "master" knows only one. Only the slave, therefore can correct defects in the consciousness of the master.[51]

The work of interpreting does not simply involve setting forth a multiplicity of meanings as expressions of conflicting life-worlds. Nor does it entail simply yielding to the voices of those who have been outsiders to us. It consists in a struggle to discover the senses in which each meaning-world relevant to a situation is true and the senses in which each may be false and misleading. So, we seek to grasp the degree to which the meaning-worlds of "others" can serve as answers to questions which are not only the questions of those others, but our questions as well. We also attempt to rethink our own meaning-worlds and to reexamine our own traditions in light of what these "others" have opened up to us. Through these inquiries, we move in quest of new and common ground, a common ground which makes fitting action possible. Gadamer speaks of this common ground as a "fusion of horizons."[52] In this frame of reference the common ground is not necessarily something already present, perhaps as a deep-level presupposition of the discourse itself. It is best to assume that the conflicts of understanding in situations of crisis are real, and that they initially reflect fundamentally different modes of worldly being. The common ground is rather a task and a hope. If it does come into being, it will be a new accomplishment, a miracle, an event of wonder, a creative transformation of difference into new harmony, rich in its contrasts. It is only the accomplishment of such a creative transformation of understanding that can lead to what is properly speaking "fitting action" in a concrete sense.

Such happy outcomes are rare given the brokenness of the human world. More often we have to "muddle through" with half-way measures, make-shift arrangements, unstable truces. We have to accept compromises which require us to endure significant levels of injustice and continuing conflict, or which perhaps leave us as accomplices and beneficiaries of such injustice and conflict. In this respect, "fitting" action as H. Richard Niebuhr defined it is in most cases not even a possibility, still less an actuality.[53] Often the best we can hope for is to arrive at those halfway measures which at least leave open the possibility of movement toward greater justice and harmony, in contrast to those which make productive advances in the future more difficult still. But this anguish is surely a characteristic of our existence "between the times."

SUMMARY AND CONCLUSION

I have been seeking to unfold what is involved in a style of moral and ethical thinking which has a distinctively historical orientation. Such an ethic centers in the attempt, as H. Richard Niebuhr put it, to interpret what is going on. Grasping what is going on, I argued, does not consist in either empirical descriptions or in scientific explanations, though both may have some relevance to the understanding we seek. It rather consists in the explication and critical appropriation of the meanings which form the lifeworlds of representative actors involved directly or indirectly in the situation we are interpreting.

I then offered a general characterization of the life-world with reference to some of its constitutive structures: intentionality, intersubjectivity, temporality, and embodiment. These structures, I claimed, order the meanings which concretely form the way "world" presents itself to us. Finally, I delineated some basic types of interpretive activity which might organize and simplify our efforts to grasp the sense of the multiplicity of meanings, and possible interpretations of those meanings, which figure in the situation we are seeking to understand. These types include the straightforward application of received conventions; suspicion of those conventions as distortions and concealments of underlying dynamics of another sort—especially dynamics tending to oppression and exploitation; and finally, the dialectical interplay between the imaginative retrieval of one's own tradition, and hospitality to the understandings of others differently oriented to the situation in question. The aim of the activity of interpreting, I suggested, is the realization of a "fusion of horizons," the imaginative production of common ground which lays the basis for the possibility of fitting action. And when common ground eludes us, as it characteristically does, our quest is to keep open constructive movement toward the wholeness it promises. For a historically oriented ethic, only personal fulfillment within a universal community of fulfillment is finally adequate to our apprehension of the good. Yet this hope is itself essentially eschatological, allowing of little more than fragmentary realizations within the ongoing movement of history.[54]

NOTES

1. Stanley Hauerwas speaks of this style of ethics as the "standard account." See his *Truthfulness and Tragedy: Further Investigations in Christian Ethics* (Notre Dame, Ind.: University of Notre Dame Press, 1977), 15–20.

2. For a useful collection of essays examining the ethical issues raised by affirmative action, see Marshall Cohen, Thomas Nagel and Thomas Scanlon, eds., *Equality and Preferential Treatment* (Princeton, N.J.: Princeton University Press, 1977). The discussion is in general governed by the quest for universalizable principles. The arguments on behalf of "preferential treatment" for oppressed minorities founder in my view because of their lack of attention to the level of abstraction which characterizes the debate as a whole.

3. I am here using the term "prejudice" in the sense developed by Gadamer, *Truth and Method*, 245.

4. Winter, *Elements for a Social Ethic*, 277.

5. Niebuhr, *Responsible Self*.

6. Ibid., 63.

7. I find useful the current distinction between moral and ethical discourse, with the former referring to "engaged" reasoning and the latter to a more reflective activity, perhaps testing the bases of concrete moral judgments. In many cases in the present study I have both levels of thinking in view, so the terms are not always kept technically distinct. I wanted, however, to avoid repeated usage of the cumbersome form "moral and ethical."

8. In fact, those engaged in empirical description scarcely think of themselves as "interpreting" at all. They are rather seeking to *avoid* interpreting and the subjectivism implied by that term. Yet my claim is that this mode of description is still a limited and determinate way of "taking" a situation, abstracting certain elements from the total meaning contexts in which they appear.

9. Of course, much of what we call social science is little more than data gathering according to precisely determined procedures. Theory is for the most part linked to method. Claims about the data take the

form of inductive generalizations or perhaps the presentation of statistical correlations. No attempt is made to "explain" the observed regularities themselves, so the apparent "necessities" underlying the data remain largely implicit.

10. In addition to Winter's own detailed attention to this problem (*Elements for a Social Ethic*, 116–212), see also Duncan McRae, Jr., *The Social Function of Social Science* (New Haven: Yale University Press, 1976).

11. See, e.g., James Gustafson, *Can Ethics Be Christian?* (Chicago: University of Chicago Press, 1975), 117–44.

12. Ibid., 124–28. The essay by Niebuhr which Gustafson has in mind is "War as Crucifixion," *The Christian Century* 60 (1943): 513–15.

13. Gustafson, *Can Ethics Be Christian?* 119.

14. I cannot document this claim fully in the present volume, especially since Gustafson lifts up four base points as important for Christian ethics: a view of the good, moral norms, agency, and the situation. Cf. especially Gustafson, "Context Versus Principles: A Misplaced Debate in Christian Ethics," in *Christian Ethics and the Community* (Philadelphia: Pilgrim Press, 1971), 101–26. The first three of these base points provide the organizing principles for his *Christ and the Moral Life* (New York: Harper & Row, 1968). All four are prominent in *Can Ethics Be Christian?* Yet in the latter volume, the first two chapters on agency (pp. 25–81) provide the basis for what follows. Likewise, in *Christ and the Moral Life*, the interpretive treatment of major thinkers in the Christian tradition issues in a discussion of categories of agency: dispositions and attitudes, intentions, beliefs, and convictions. Similarly, in *The Contributions of Theology to Medical Ethics* (Milwaukee: Marquette University Press, 1975) the theological motifs which are discussed, mainly relating to a doctrine of God, are explicated in terms of certain attitudes considered appropriate for Christian actors: respect for life, openness, self-criticism. I am suggesting, in short, that the creative center of Gustafson's constructive work lies in the area of agency.

Stanley Hauerwas captures and continues this central feature in Gustafson's thought, though Hauerwas is self-conscious about the fact that the notion of character is not merely one theme among others, but a privileged entrée into the total sweep of Christian ethics. Cf. *Truthfulness and Tragedy*, 1–2. The systematic development which Hauerwas gives the notion of character reduces the "subjectivist" feel of Gustafson's writings. See my review of Hauerwas's writings. "Character and Narrative: A Review Essay of Stanley Hauerwas's Studies of the Christian Life," *Religious Studies Review* 6/1 (January 1980): 25–30.

15. Hauerwas has recently given special attention to this matter in *Truthfulness and Tragedy*, 11–12, 82–100.

16. On this point, see Ricoeur, *The Voluntary and the Involuntary*, Eng. trans. Kohák, 72–77. See also chap. 3 in this volume, "The Relation of Values to Human Need."

17. I see a certain dominance to this style of thinking in recent American Christian ethics. It appears, e.g., in the writings of Paul Ramsey, Gene Outka, Ralph Potter, James Childress, Glen Stassen, and others. For clear examples, see the recent focus on Christian social ethics in the *Journal of Religious Ethics* (Spring 1977).

18. Cf., e.g., Paul Ramsey, *The Ethics of Fetal Research* (New Haven, Conn.: Yale University Press, 1975), 31–36.

19. Cf. Paul Ramsey, *The Just War: Force and Political Responsibility* (New York: Charles Scribner's Sons, 1968).

20. Cf. especially Kant, *Critique of Practical Reason*, 137–39.

21. The phrase is taken from Hauerwas, *Truthfulness and Tragedy*, 1. As I have indicated, however, I believe it reflects the central logic of Gustafson's position.

22. Husserl, *The Crisis of European Sciences and Transcendental Phenomenology*, 137–41, 379–83.

23. Edmund Husserl, "Phenomenology," Eng. trans. Richard E. Palmer, *Encyclopaedia Britannica* (1927), 88–89.

24. While I cannot in this essay display the force of the claim, I believe that the phenomenology of the life-world also permits us to overcome, or at least to reformulate in a more satisfactory manner, the troublesome dichotomies that have often hampered modern ethical thought: fact and value, the "is" and the "ought," the indicative and the imperative, objectivity and subjectivity, reason and feeling, and so on.

25. Assimilating Husserl's notion of the life-world to Martin Heidegger's notion of "being-in-the-world" is problematic. Husserl's interest was primarily epistemological; Heidegger's, ontological. I suspect that Heidegger's existentialist thrust is finally of more immediate interest to the student of ethics. See *Being and Time*, 78–90. Yet Husserl's studies are not in my reading incompatible with this accent. Indeed, Husserl may serve ethical inquiry more directly in relating normative understandings of social reality to human science perspectives. In this latter task Alfred Schutz's continuation of Husserl's inquiries with particular reference to the human sciences is also quite important for social ethics. Cf. especially his *Collected Papers*, 1: 3–66, and also Schutz and Luckman, *Structures of the Life-World*, 3–98.

26. Cf. Schutz, *Collected Papers*, 1: 15–19.

27. Husserl, *Cartesian Meditations*, 71–148. Cf. also Husserl, *The Crisis of European Sciences and Transcendental Phenomenology*, 3–18.

28. For discussions of temporality in relation to the moral life, see Howard L. Harrod, "Interpreting and Projecting: Two Elements of the Self as Moral Agent," *Journal of the American Academy of Religion* 41/1 (March 1973): 18–29, and H. Ganse Little, *Decision and Responsibility: A Wrinkle in Time* (Missoula, Mont.: Scholars Press, 1974).

29. Schutz, *Collected Papers*, 1: 307.

30. On embodiment, see Richard Zaner, *The Problem of Embodiment: Some Contributions to a Phenomenology of the Body* (The Hague: Martinus Nijhoff, 1971), especially pp. 250–61.

31. Schutz, *Collected Papers*, 1: 227.

32. Niebuhr, *Responsible Self*, 61–65.

33. Niebuhr, *Responsible Self*, 65. The accent on sociality coheres nicely with Niebuhr's call for a "relational theory of values." See his essay, "The Center of Value," in *Radical Monotheism and Western Culture*, 100–13.

34. Winter, *Elements for a Social Ethic*, 85–118.

35. Ibid., 137.

36. Ibid., 141–56.

37. Ibid., 264–79. Winter has carried out these operations in his little monograph, *Being Free: Reflections on America's Cultural Revolution* (New York: Macmillan, 1966).

38. Heidegger, *Being and Time*, 185.

39. Gadamer, *Truth and Method*, 416.

40. Heidegger, *Being and Time*, 190, 192.

41. Ibid., 195.

42. Niebuhr, *Responsible Self*, 122–26. Cf. also "The Center of Value," op. cit.

43. Schutz, *Collected Papers*, 1: 13–14.

44. Ricoeur, *Freud and Philosophy*, 32–36.

45. Ricoeur, *The Conflict of Interpretations: Essays in Hermeneutics*, ed. Don Ihde (Evanston, Ill.: Northwestern University Press, 1974), 23.

46. Ricoeur, *Freud and Philosophy*, 28–32.

47. For my development of this motif as a paradigm for interpreting moral experience, see chap. 2, "Hospitality to the Stranger," in the present volume.

48. Many other thinkers share this general orientation, most notably Ernst Troeltsch. For my study of Troeltsch, see *Christian Faith and History: A Critical Comparison of Ernst Troeltsch and Karl Barth* (Nashville: Abingdon Press, 1965).

More recently, this general style can be seen in the writings of James Sellers, especially his *Public Ethics* (New York: Macmillan, 1970), and Robert Bellah, e.g., *The Broken Covenant* (New York: Seabury Press, 1973).

49. Winter, *Being Free*, 138–43.

50. Gadamer, *Truth and Method*, 245–46.

51. G. F. W. Hegel, *The Phenomenology of Mind*, Eng. trans. J. B. Baillie (London: George Allen & Unwin, 1931), 234–40. Similar insights can be found in W. E. B. Dubois's notion of the "double consciousness" of black Americans and in Karl Marz's claims about the privileged status of the proletarian orientation to social reality and its contradictions. For the former, see *The Souls of Black Folk*, reprinted in *Three Negro Clas-*

sics, ed. John Hope Franklin (New York: Avon Books, 1965), 213–21. For the latter, see *Economic and Philosophic Manuscripts of 1844* (New York: International Publishers, 1964), 159ff. Dubois's accent is on the pain of "double consciousness," the consciousness of being both Negro and American. Yet in another frame of reference this pain becomes a resource for criticism.

52. Gadamer, *Truth and Method*, 237.

53. H. Richard Niebuhr defines the fitting as follows:

> Thus our responsive actions have the character of fittingness or unfittingness. We seek to make them fit into a process of interaction. The questions we raise about them are not only those of their rightness or wrongness, their goodness or badness, but of their fitness or unfittingness in the total movement, the whole conversation. We seek to have them fit into the whole as a sentence fits into a paragraph in a book, a note into a chord in a movement in a symphony, as the act of eating a common meal fits into the lifelong companionship of a family, as the decision of a statesman fits into the ongoing movement of his nation's life with other nations, or as the discovery of a scientific verifact fits into the history of science.
>
> *The Responsible Self*, 97.

54. These notions are taken from the thought of Paul Tillich, e.g., *Love, Power and Justice* (New York: Oxford University Press, 1954), 124, and *Systematic Theology*, 3: 138–41, 406–08.

5

THE ESCHATOLOGICAL HORIZON
OF NEW TESTAMENT
SOCIAL THOUGHT

The New Testament is a puzzle for students of Christian social ethics. On the one hand, we note the explosive character of many New Testament motifs: Jesus' announcement of the presence of the coming kingdom of God with dramatic signs and mighty deeds; his summons to followers to break loose from traditional life patterns in order to devote their lives to that kingdom; or the Pauline celebration of the freedom and oneness of all people in Jesus Christ. These themes suggest the possibility of an innovative socio-political vision. On the other hand, explicit New Testament statements about the basic institutions of society— household, state, economy—are disappointingly tame. For the most part, the eschatological people are counseled to adjust themselves to the prevailing arrangements in these primary spheres of human life.

Given such mixed signals in the New Testament texts, it is not surprising that there is relatively little consensus in Christian social thought. From almost unqualified allegiance to existing social orders to revolutionary transformations of these orders, virtually every conceivable approach to social existence has received significant development and advocacy by interpreters of Christian faith. I shall not venture to reduce this diversity in Christian social thought. Its most interesting features reflect the fact that Christian social thought takes account of variable situational factors in its analyses and proposals, precluding in advance a general and definitive set of understandings. My aim is rather to locate more precisely the social radicalism and institutional creativity which does appear in the New Testament and to suggest how themes in these texts might contribute to original social thought.[1] I shall chiefly have in view the Synoptic Gospels and the authentic Pauline letters (1 Thessalonians, Galatians, 1 and 2 Corinthians, Romans, Philippians, and Philemon). For the purposes of this paper, these texts are illustrative of an approach, though I do believe that they provide the richest resource for Christian social ethics.

The basic thesis is that the radicalism and creativity of New Testament social thought relate chiefly to the internal dynamics of the community of faith. They express the struggle of early Christian leaders to work out forms of common life appropriate to the gospel. Distinctively Christian social thought most appropriately takes its bearings from these efforts. New Testament treatments of the state or of economic activity are in comparison relatively uninteresting. For all practical purposes New Testament authors and redactors take the existing arrangements in these spheres of life as more or less given. They perceive these arrangements as largely external to their primary activities, and as effectively beyond their social reach. These basic institutions belong to the old age which is passing away. In this respect their status has been rendered equivocal. They have relevance only for an interim between the dawning of the new age and its final consummation. In the interim, these social structures do continue to enjoy provisional legitimacy. Except in cases where they make idolatrous claims (e.g., Revelation 13), Christians are admonished to acknowledge them and to live within the constraints they set.[2] A Christian social ethic which proceeds from these materials will have little to say of substantive importance on political and economic questions.

THE PRIMACY OF
ESCHATOLOGICAL COMMUNITY

The key to Synoptic and Pauline social thought is their distinctive eschatology. The central premise is that the coming new age is already taking form in the world and that the present evil age is passing away, though its institutions persist for the time being. The two ages are dialectically related. In some respects those who respond to the gospel are wholly subject to the claims of the new age. They abide by its ground rules. They already are an eschatological people living with one another in a new kind

128

of human community. In other respects they remain under the dominion of the old age, acknowledging the provisional validity of its institutions. This dialectic thrusts them into conflict with their wider social world. They experience suffering and persecution at the hands of those who resist the reality of the new age.[3]

The most crucial point is that the emerging communities of faith displace the family as the foundational social unit. In ancient Israel and early Judaism, the family was an integral feature of covenant existence. The covenant linked clans and tribes together to form a people, and the well-being of the people depended upon the propagation and socialization of offspring. For the early Christian communities the family is quite secondary, enjoying no essential role in eschatological existence. The well-being of the communities depends rather upon an evangelistic witness and upon the successful incorporation of converts from many nations into a viable community life.

"Who are my mother and my brothers?" Jesus asks. "Whoever does the will of God is my brother and sister and mother" (Mark 3:33, 35; cf. Matt. 12:46–50, Luke 8:19–20). And later: "Truly, I say to you, there is no one who has left house or brothers or sisters or mother or father or children or lands, for my sake and for the gospel, who will not receive a hundredfold now in this time, houses and brothers and sisters and mothers and children and lands, with persecutions, and in the age to come, eternal life" (Mark 10:29–30; cf. Matt. 19:27–30, Luke 18:28–30). The household that matters is the household of faith, a gathered community from the nations of the world.

Paul likewise relativizes family relationships and subordinates them to the community of faith. In eschatological community, singleness is not simply a tolerable deviation from the norm; it has positive advantages. Married persons, Paul notes, must hold in view the needs of the partner and other household members. The single person is free to focus total attention on the promises and imperatives of the gospel and to persevere without equivocation in the face of the hardships accompanying Christian mission (1 Cor. 7:25–28). The Christian community does not maintain itself through children born to Christian families; it lives by mission. Its basis is not blood but faith, and faith comes in response to the preaching of the gospel. This move opens the way to fellowship in Christ among persons of different races, ethnic communities, and social classes. It is a precondition for the recognition of the equality of men and women. It underlies the Christian sense of a global reach and of an inclusive human community. In these respects it has altogether radical implications.

THE JEWISH LEGACY
IN SYNOPTIC ACCOUNTS OF
ESCHATOLOGICAL EXISTENCE

The accomplishment of eschatological existence requires a rethinking of classic Jewish traditions. On the one hand, the Christian movement is profoundly dependent on the Jewish legacy, even in the gentile world. On the other hand, that legacy gains new meaning in the eschatological context of early Christian thought. The surface issues are the status of community-maintaining ritual patterns: circumcision, food laws, sabbath observances, and, to a lesser extent, temple sacrifices. These patterns are recurring occasions of overt conflict between faithful Jews and the new Christians.[4] The underlying problem, which Paul and the Synoptic authors see clearly, is the role of law in eschatological community.

Mark's Gospel breaks most completely with Judaism. Jewish ritual patterns are set aside in favor of distinctively Christian practices, and the continuity with Israel is restricted to the moral features of law and prophets. Note in this connection Mark's treatment of the two great commandments. The point for Mark is that the love commandments are "much more than all whole burnt offerings and sacrifices" (Mark 12:32–33).

Luke-Acts displays the strongest continuity with Judaism. For Luke the gentile Christian community is founded upon the prior gathering of a repentant Israel. For Jew and gentile alike, the laws and ordinances of God are binding, though in variant ways. Gentile Christians are accountable to the law in a fashion analogous to that of "strangers" living among the Jews in ancient Palestine. They are not obliged to submit to circumcision or to the full range of food laws. They are to "abstain from the pollutions of idols and from unchastity and from what is strangled and from blood" (Acts 15:19–21; cf. Lev. 17–18). Otherwise, full compliance with the dictates of the law is an obligation for gentile as well as Jewish Christians. Even Paul is portrayed by Luke as the pious Pharisee faithfully obeying the law to the end (e.g., Acts 28:17, 23).[5]

For Luke the primary import of eschatology is that the classic concerns of law and prophets for the poor, the outcast, the stranger, the blind, and the lame take on new reality and urgency. Jesus' critique of the Pharisees, scribes, and Sadducees is not that they misunderstand the law or elevate their traditions above the divine commands. It is that they do not fully observe what the law requires, especially with regard to almsgiving or compassion for the poor, the blind and the lame, tax-collectors and "sinners."[6]

Liberation theology heightens our awareness of the dramatic reversals of fortune among rich and poor, the powerful and the lowly, celebrated in early Christian hymns and incorporated into the opening chapters of Luke's Gospel (e.g., the "Magnificat," Luke 1:51–53; and the "Nunc Dimittis," Luke 2:34–35). In the same vein, redaction criticism enables us to appreciate more fully the thematic centrality of Jesus' citation of Isaiah's great oracle of liberation in Luke 4:16–21.

> The Spirit of the Lord is upon me, because he has annointed me to preach good news to the poor; he has sent me to proclaim release to the captives and recovering of sight to the blind, to set at liberty those who are oppressed, to proclaim the acceptable year of the Lord.
>
> (cf. Isa. 61:1–2)

This oracle sets forth the "platform" of Jesus' ministry. The narrative which follows displays its concrete fulfillment in Jesus' words and deeds (Luke 4:21, 4:31—7:23). The point is driven home in Jesus' response to the query of the disciples of John the Baptist: "Are you he who is to come; or shall we look for another?" "Go and tell John what you have seen and heard," Jesus replies. "The blind receive their sight, the lame walk, lepers are cleansed, and the deaf hear, the dead are raised up, the poor have good news preached to them" (Luke 7:22).

When we examine Luke-Acts for clues to the social impact of these dramatic themes, what we find falls short of a revolutionary reversal of basic social institutions. The outcome is the emergence of a community of faith which embraces outcasts and social outsiders, and gathers people from among the nations. This community, however, is made up of persons who have distinctive attitudes toward property. They no longer clutch at property. In response to the claims of the kingdom they are free to let goods and property go and to place them at the disposal of others in need. Luke makes this orientation concrete in terms of two practices: almsgiving and communal property. The former is more pervasive in Luke-Acts; the latter appears only in the early chapters of Acts in reports of what Luke treats as a short-lived experiment unique to the Jerusalem church (Acts 2:43–47, 4:32, 34–37; cf. Acts 5:1–11, 6:1–6). Almsgiving discloses freedom with respect to property; the community of goods, its social nature. Almsgiving also expresses a social orientation to property, though less unequivocally. What one has acquired is no longer simply one's own to dispose of as one sees fit. It exists for the well-being of the community as a whole. It establishes communal bonds with the poor and the outcast.[7]

John Howard Yoder argues that these materials constitute a specific socio-political option, one which makes direct claims upon contemporary Christian communities.[8] If we follow his argument, we need to keep in view the fragmentary nature of this option. Luke gives no attention to questions related to the production of the means of subsistence, nor to any mechanisms for distributing what is produced. He simply accepts existing arrangements for handling such matters despite their link with the old age. He assumes that Christians will continue to participate in established economic structures in securing their livelihood, though certain kinds of activities would doubtless be excluded, for example, tax-collecting and usury. What he describes are individual and communal commitments to redistribute for the well-being of the community the resources gained through participation in the economic structures of the time. It is unlikely that Christian communities could maintain such patterns over time without developing them a good deal further, for example, by devising ways within the community to approximate economic self sufficiency at the level of production, or by defining more precisely the limits of the obligation to give alms and by making clear the obligation of all to contribute as they are able to community well-being. Without moves of this sort the Lukan "option" could hardly resist the shaping power of the dominant economic institutions of the ancient world.

I would suggest that the importance of Luke-Acts for social ethics is rather that it opens the question of the material basis of eschatological community. Eschatological community is community in which status and class distinctions are abolished. All believers are numbered among the poor, the hungry, the sorrowful, and the despised for whom the gospel comes as good news. This insight, deeply rooted in the prophetic tradition, provides an impulse to work toward institutional arrangements congruent with the equality of the people of God. To address the realities of the modern world, such arrangements cannot simply be lifted out of first-century contexts. Their realization requires a productive imagination informed by concrete social experience and by an adequate theoretical grasp of forces at work in that world. Their impulse is against individualistic conceptions of property and in favor of social understandings. Property exists for the corporate well-being of the people. The task for social ethics is to construct viable ways of institutionalizing that impulse.

On the question of law and tradition, Matthew stands between Mark and Luke. Like Luke, Matthew's Jesus insists upon the continuing authority of the whole of the Mosiac law: ". . . till heaven and earth pass away, not an iota, not a dot, will pass away" (Matt. 5:18). In contrast to Luke, Matthew envisions a fundamental reinterpretation of the law. For Matthew's Jesus, law essentially concerns the perfection of love. Thus, the two great commandments, love for God and neighbor, are the foundation of the whole law. Upon them depend ("hang," *krematai*) all the law and the prophets (Matt. 22:36–40).

Matthew does not treat the love commandments as sufficient guides to the will of God, such that one might dispense with all other laws and traditions. He is as troubled by antinomianism as by formalism.[9] His regard for the law reflects a belief that the law is divine revelation, and as such, eternally binding. His procedure is not to deal with individual situations in terms of the love commandments alone, viewed in abstraction from the richness of the legal traditions; it is to approach situations by way of the teachings of law and prophets, interpreting these materials in terms of the love commandments. The full sweep of the law is operative, but it is read as commanding love. Matthew thus maintains the continuity of tradition while providing a way to reassess and reinterpret it in changing social and cultural situations.

There are two important ingredients in Matthew's handling of Jesus' teachings on the law. First, obedience to the law involves not simply correct behavior, but the full investment of the total self. It encompasses subjective intentions, attitudes and feelings, and the workings of the imagination. Matthew not only lifts up the love command as the interpretive clue to the meaning of the law; guided by that command he suggests a new way of conceiving what is entailed in obeying the law in the first place. Fundamental attitudes and feelings figure in our commitment to observe all that has been commanded.[10]

Second, the obedience of faith entails radical vulnerability to adversaries. To be a disciple is to be at odds with the social order; it is to be subject to persecution. One is not to respond to persecutors in kind, however, for to meet violence with violence and to repay injury with injury is to remain embroiled in the cycle of destruction characteristic of the old order. Something new is coming into being, a community of love and mercy. Matthew's Jesus provides an account of what is required if the new form of community is to maintain itself in face of pressure from the old order: a capacity to absorb the violence of that order without recompense. One submits to the power and authority of the old order, but refuses its confidence in violence as a means for achieving individual and social ends.

The social import of Matthew's interpretation of the law is most explicit in his treatment of mercy and forgiveness within the community of faith. Mercy for Matthew is virtually equivalent to love (e.g., Matt. 12:7, 23:23). Its importance is underscored by the fact that the petition for the forgiveness of debts is the only phrase of the Lord's prayer singled out for comment: "If you forgive others their trespasses, your heavenly Father will also forgive you; but if you do not forgive others, neither will your Father forgive you" (Matt. 6:14, au. trans.).

What is here of primary interest is that Matthew reports a procedure for institutionalizing forgiveness within the church as a way of resolving conflicts and maintaining community in spite of the inevitable hurts people inflict upon one another. If someone wrongs me, I am first to take steps to work things out with that person, alone and in private. If that fails, I am to bring one or two witnesses into the process. If their attempts at mediation fail, the dispute goes to the whole church for adjudication, with the possibility that the offending parties might be expelled for violating the conditions of eschatological community (Matt. 18:15–20). There is no talk here of turning the other cheek or of going the second mile. In addressing disputes internal to the community of faith, the primary considerations are justice and mercy.

Matthew's account of these formal procedures is followed by two pericopes dealing with forgiveness: Jesus' admonition to Peter to forgive the brother (or sister) who sins against him, if need be, as many as seventy times seven (Matt. 18:22), and the parable of the unforgiving servant (Matt. 18:23–35). As these texts suggest, the desired outcome of efforts to resolve disputes within the community is not the expulsion of offending parties, but forgiveness and reconciliation.

In Matthew's thought, human community is not constituted by kinship or nationality, nor by a common language and culture, still less by violence; it is founded on mercy—mutual forbearance and forgiveness. Such mercy has its basis in the mercy of God. It presupposes a prior commitment to discipleship, a readiness to "do all things whatsoever" Jesus commands. It is the commitment to Jesus as Lord which binds the disciples together; it is their willingness to forgive one another which enables them to stay together. Through these themes we gain suggestions about the conditions of a public order among diverse peoples who on the basis of natural associations would not normally have any possibility of a common life.[11] No more than Luke does Matthew provide us with a comprehensive way of thinking about social order. We get fragments and indications stemming from experiences in the early Christian communities. Yet these fragments and indications generate impulses to create a public life within communities which transcend nationality, language, and culture.

PAULINE ESCHATOLOGY AND
SOCIAL AND CULTURAL RELATIVITY

In comparison with the Synoptic authors, Paul both challenges most radically the central thrust of the Jewish legacy and also maintains the strongest sense of linkage to the ongoing Jewish community. The occasion for his reflections is the gentile mission and his attempts to promote fellowship among Jewish and Gentile converts. The immediate difficulties concern circumcision and the food laws. Must Gentiles be circumcised as a condition for entry into eschatological community? Is table fellowship possible among observant Jews and gentile converts? (Galatians 2). An analogous problem is raised by the scruples of gentile converts over the eating of meat prepared in the context of hellenistic sacrificial rites (1 Corinthians 8). Do such rites link the eating of meat to idol worship? Must meat be shunned, therefore, by the faithful?

In response to both sets of problems Paul claims that the gospel relativizes all human traditions. What counts is Christian freedom in Christ and the building up of community in him. In Christ one is free to accept the traditions and institutions that previously have ordered life, provided their relativity is fully understood and provided they do not interfere with the realization of community. "Neither circumcision counts for anything nor uncircumcision, but keeping the commandments of God," Paul contends (1 Cor. 7:19). The male Jew is a person in Christ as circumcised; the male gentile, as uncircumcised. The food laws could not be allowed to stand in quite the same fashion since their strict observance was a barrier to fellowship. Consequently, Jewish Christians had to modify or let go of these traditions, except perhaps in the privacy of their homes. New rituals emerged to express the corporate reality of an inclusive human community: Baptism, the Lord's supper, and love feasts.

Paul's assessment of the eating of meat offered to idols parallels his treatment of the dispute about circumcision. "Food will not commend us to God. We are no worse off if we do not eat, and no better off if we do" (1 Cor. 8:8). The imperative is to avoid jeopardizing the community of faith. "Knowledge puffs up," he observes, "but love builds up" (1 Cor. 8:1).

For Paul, no particular cultural patterns are requisite to Christian existence; nor are any excluded unless they hinder freedom and community in Christ. Freedom from all determinate social and cultural forms is also freedom to accept all as provisionally valid provided they are subject to the conditions of freedom. In Christ we have died to the old self and entered into the liberty of the children of God; therefore, we have access to all human ways. Indeed, we embrace them for the sake of Christ. "Though I am free from all human ways," Paul asserts, "I have made myself a slave to all, that I might win the more" (1 Cor. 9:19). He continues:

> To the Jews I became as a Jew, in order to win Jews; to those under the law I became as one under the law—though not being myself under the law—that I might win those under the law. To those outside the law I became as one outside the law—not being without law toward God but under the law [i.e., *nomos*, or principle] of Christ—that I might win those outside the law. To the weak I became weak, that I might win the weak. I have become all things to all [people], that I might by all means save some. I do it all for the sake of the gospel, that I may share in its blessings.
>
> (1 Cor. 9:20–23)

Paul is not saying, "everything is permitted." He is contrasting the relativity of human cultures with the foundational understandings of the gospel. The gospel permits us to celebrate pluralism and welcome it into the community of faith. Jewish Christians can remain Jewish provided they appreciate the relativity of Jewish patterns and observe them in a fashion which does not divide, but rather builds up and enriches the whole people of God. On the same terms, gentile Christians can remain gentile. Paul is pointing to forms of fellowship which allow for ritual differences among the people of God.[12]

The recognition of cultural relativity and pluralism rests upon Paul's reassessment of the place of law in the activity of God. In his reading of the gospel, the righteousness of God has become manifest in Jesus Christ apart from the law. Law belongs to childhood (Gal. 4:1–7) and slavery (Gal. 4:21–31). It was added because of transgressions, till the offspring should come to whom the promise was made (Gal. 3:19). That offspring is Jesus Christ, though Jesus Christ also embraces all who place their trust in him. Pointedly stated, Christ is the end of the law (Rom. 10:4). The term "end" (*telos*) conveys a sense of fullfillment. Insofar as the law is holy and just and good, its intent has been realized in Jesus Christ. Yet the dominant sense is that of annulment. The law has no more significance for those who live by faith in Jesus Christ.

In place of law stands promise. Promise specifies an unconditional and open-ended commitment of persons to one another.

It refers in the first instance to the activity of God on behalf of the people of God, but it embraces as well the mutual commitments and obligations of the people to one another. Promise is given face to face. It concerns the concrete dynamics of human interactions. Law is intermediate. It stands between parties to a relationship and regulates their interactions. "It was ordained by angels," Paul suggests, and it was given through an "intermediary" (Gal. 3:19). As intermediate, law calls attention to itself and demands respect for itself even though it claims to serve the relationships it regulates. In Paul's view it is secondary to promise and more abstract than promise. Promise is oriented to the future. It takes account of the continual need of communities engaged in mission to rethink and renegotiate the terms of their common life. Such renegotiation is essential if persons coming from different backgrounds are to be fully incorporated into the growing communities of faith. Law is oriented to the past. It accents the cumulative experiences and wisdom of the past, though it includes the possibility of adapting past learnings to more or less novel situations. Law gives stability to human relationships while promise highlights their creation and renewal. Where promise is fully operative, Paul contends, law is irrelevant. Promise enables the accomplishment of mutually supportive and mutually enriching communal relationships in a manner that law as such is incapable of doing.[13]

Paul interprets Israel's own pilgrimage in terms of promise. Israel's identity stems not from fidelity to the commandments of God offered at Sinai, but from trust in the promises of God given to Abraham. Abraham, not Moses, is the central figure in Israelite life (cf. Gal. 3:15–18; Rom. 4:13–24). The promises of God express the righteousness of God which is bestowed upon human beings apart from the law, though, as Paul notes, law and prophets bear witness to it. Law has indeed been prominent in Israel. It is, moreover, good. It contains the oracles of God. Yet its primary function is not to establish Israel as God's covenant people, but to give knowledge of sin (e.g., Rom. 3:20, 7:7). It came in, Paul argues, because of trespasses. In Jesus Christ the power of sin has been broken, and the promise to Abraham has once again become effective apart from the law. Thus, while Matthew's Jesus offers a reinterpretation of the law as essentially commanding love, Paul offers a reinterpretation of the legacy of Israel in terms of promise rather than law.

If Israel's life stems from promise, Paul reasons, then Israel's heritage is available to the nations apart from the law. "We hold," Paul says, "that a person is justified by faith apart from works of the law." "Is God a God of Jews only?" he continues. "Is he not the God of the Gentiles also? Yes, of Gentiles also since God is one. God will justify the circumcised on the grounds of their faith, and the uncircumcised through faith" (Rom. 3:28–31). Paul's acknowledgement of the relativity of human cultures and his ability to build community across cultural and ethnic lines are of a piece with his insight into the primacy of promise over law. This insight permits cultural pluralism in the community of faith.

Paul's understanding of cultural relativity is most fully developed with respect to Jewish and hellenistic ritual patterns. It concerns openness to the gentile mission and fellowship between Jew and gentile in the community of faith. Yet Paul also senses some of the implications of his basic position for other social relations. Of special interest is his consideration of the bearing of the gospel on the status of women and slaves. He affirms that women and men, slave and free, are one in Christ Jesus, in parallel with the unity of Jew and gentile (Gal. 3:28). The gentile mission is directed to individuals and not households. Women and slaves are free, therefore, to enter Christian community on equal terms with free men and without the sanction of the patriarchal head of the household.[14] Paul advises women converts to grant divorces to unbelieving spouses who request them and to separate themselves from the household. Still, his counsel is that everyone should remain in the state in which he or she was called (1 Cor. 7:20, 24). With regard to slaves, this admonition is explicit. "Were you a slave when called? Never mind. But if you can gain your freedom, avail yourself of the opportunity. For he who was called in the Lord as a slave is a freeman of the Lord. Likewise, he who was free when called is a slave of Christ" (1 Cor. 7:21–22). Paul's position parallels his observations on circumcision and the eating of meat.

In Paul's authentic letters we do not find an analogous statement on the status of women in the household.[15] Were he to continue in the same vein, however, we could expect him to say something like the following: "Neither the patriarchal nor the egalitarian household counts for anything, but abiding in the promises of God." Or perhaps: "Equality in the household will not commend you to God. You will be no worse off if you remain subordinate to your husband, and no better off were you to enjoy equal standing. Your true freedom and your full equality are in Jesus Christ." Paul's underlying conviction is that all patterns of household organization are relative to particular social contexts. No patterns as such are essential to Christian existence, and none is alien unless it undermines the conditions of freedom and community in Christ. This orientation could be extended to political and economic systems as well, though Paul does not explicitly pursue the possibility (cf. 1 Cor. 7:29–31).

Paul's treatment of household relations is sound enough so long as we have in view only the circumstances of subordinate members. Christians are to "have the mind of Christ" and to empty themselves in service to others (Phil. 2:5–7); they can, therefore, accept subordinate status in household, state, and society without compromising their freedom in Christ. This stance becomes problematic when we have in view Christian households, or perhaps Christian patriarchs and Christian slaveholders. It is not apparent that a slaveholder who in Christ receives his slave "as more than a slave and as a beloved brother" can continue exercising unilateral dominion over that slave in the household (cf. Philemon, v. 16). Similarly, the believing husband who recognizes his oneness with his wife in Jesus Christ cannot, it would seem, remain her master. Within the community of faith, the standard pattern is mutuality and reciprocity in service: ". . . through love be servants of one another" (Gal. 5:13); "bear one another's burdens . . ." (Gal. 6:2); "do nothing from selfishness or conceit, but in humility count others better than yourselves; look not only to your own interests, but also to the interests of others" (Phil. 2:3–4). If the same reciprocity were not to carry over into Christian households or to the self-understandings of Christian husbands and slaveholders, then the hierarchy of the household would insinuate itself once more into the community of faith itself, undermining the equality and unity which belong to its essential make-up.

This result unfolds in the New Testament itself. Compare Paul's accomplishments with the Deutero-Pauline epistles (Colossians and Ephesians) and the pastoral epistles (1 Timothy and Titus). Paul's recognition of the relativity of household arrangements gives way in Colossians and Ephesians to a christological defense of the patriarchal family (Col. 3:18—4:1; Eph. 5:22—6:8; cf. 1 Pet. 2:13—3:7).[16] In the pastorals the subordination of women in the household is generalized to the totality of the Christian life including the church. The circle is complete when an editor of Paul's Corinthian correspondence inserts passages which counter the themes or 1 Corinthians 7 with thinking more in line with the viewpoint of the pastorals (1 Cor. 11:3–16; 14:34–36).

The difficulty does not lie with Paul's basic orientation—the relativity of all cultural patterns and institutional forms and the freedom of Christians to participate in those forms so long as they do not violate the conditions of freedom. The difficulty is in distinguishing relatively benign social and cultural patterns from those which endanger freedom and community in Christ. The analogy for assessing the patriarchal household is not the more or less indifferent practice of circumcision, nor the eating of meat offered to idols. It is the community-hindering dietary practices of Jewish Christians in Galatia. Just as the Jewish food laws had to be set aside for the sake of full fellowship with gentiles, so the patriarchal household needed to be reordered and transformed for the sake of communion between male and female, slave and free.

Despite his shortcomings in thinking through the logic of his position, Paul's contributions to social thought remain profound. He discloses the transiency and relativity of all social arrangements and cultural patterns. None can be exalted to finality, and quite a wide range of human ways can be embraced in Christian freedom. The primary considerations are always the maintenance of Christian freedom and the building up of Christian community. This stance allows for a global orientation and it serves the quest for a common humanity amid the plurality of cultures and social institutions. At the same time, it provides a critical principle for assessing both culture and society in the forward-moving dynamics of history.

ESCHATOLOGY AND SOCIAL ETHICS

What kind of social ethic might be generated by these materials? My thesis is that the radicalism and creativity of New Testament

141

social thought chiefly concern the internal dynamics of the community of faith. They stem from attempts to devise forms of communal life appropriate to eschatological existence. Institutions basic to the larger society—especially the state and the economic order—are largely external to that undertaking. They belong to the old age which is passing away. They continue to enjoy provisional validity so long as that age persists, and Christians should in general respect them and abide by their terms. The primary energies of Christians are devoted, however, to eschatological existence within communities of faith.

The point to note is that there is nothing intrinsic to eschatological community which dictates that it remain small and marginal, confined to the private sector in larger human societies. On the contrary, eschatological existence is essentially evangelistic. It has a promise to deliver to the nations. The possibility is always present that the dynamics of eschatological existence will set in motion transformative social processes in spheres of life which previously were almost wholly independent of its central impulses. I have already noted this movement in the case of Paul's treatment of the household. Changes in status within the community of faith imply changes in household relationships among participants in that community. Paul's failure to appreciate the import of such changes was probably a factor in the subsequent restoration of patriarchy within the community of faith itself. If we hold fast to the central claim that Christ has overcome the distinction and opposition among male and female, slave and free, then we are obliged to rework the structure of Christian households to conform to this new reality. Only by doing so do we clearly maintain the primacy of eschatological community. And once households are reordered, the stage is set for analogous changes in other spheres of social existence.

A distinctively Christian social ethic which reaches beyond concerns internal to self-concious communities of faith pre-supposes situations in which the dynamics of eschatological existence are beginning to work themselves out in wider spheres of social life. Once these dynamics are underway, we are in a position to consider the broader social ramifications of elemental discoveries in the community of faith itself. Apart from this state of affairs, any substantive treatments of ethical issues intrinsic to basic social institutions will more appropriately be informed

142

by moral traditions more or less independent of Christian faith, perhaps on the basis of permission derived from that faith. They will not derive their authority from understandings ingredient in the gospel message.

Any effective development of the broader social import of the Christian message will itself have to bring into play the constructive imagination of the contemporary interpreter. "Biblical realism" is not a realistic possibility. Biblical ethics is not yet Christian social ethics, though it may be an important resource for the latter. Understanding requires us to grasp in a new setting, one considerably more complex, the force of eschatological promise for the social organization of life. Themes which merit our thoughtful attention and our practical struggle would seem to include the following:

1. The primacy of eschatological community over the family opens the way to communities which are inclusive of racial and ethnic diversity, which allow and even value singleness, and which affirm the full equality of men and women. Where the family remains foundational to social order, communities and societies can grow only through family growth, or through confederations and alliances among families in which family ties retain their associational centrality. Mark and Paul are most explicit about the changed status of the family in Christian eschatology. Paul develops the implications of this change for concrete communal relationships. This development does not nullify the family, but it bestows on the family a new social location which requires some rethinking of its status in human life. A social ethic based on this elemental accomplishment commits us to the quest for communities and societies which are racially, ethnically, and sexually inclusive.

2. Luke directs attention to the material basis of eschatological community. The dawning age leads to the reversal of existing patterns of privilege, power, and wealth in human community, or better, it leads to the obliteration of these distinctions. Our response to the claims of the kingdom involves our freedom with respect to property. That same freedom permits us to apprehend its communal meaning, to place property at the disposal of fellow human beings who have need of it, especially within the household of faith. As a social policy, this vision is limited in Luke-Acts to a voluntary redistribution of what individuals have gained

143

for personal consumption through their participation in the processes of production and exchange in the larger society. Yet it creates matrices of experience within which a more encompassing grasp of social possibilities can emerge, one which gives reality to a social understanding of property. It may be too much to claim that this vision entails socialism in the modern sense, at least not without a good deal of qualification; even so, the vision invites us to consider socialism as an appropriate way of institutionalizing the social nature of property. It more clearly constitutes a critique of the individualism and acquisitiveness of modern capitalist societies. It points to social accountability and social use in property relations and in economic activity.

3. Matthew directs our attention to the conditions of a public life in communities and societies where nationality and culture are being transcended as bases of social order and where violence is resisted as the final court of appeal in the adjudication of human conflict. The gospel highlights shared commitments, mutual forbearance, and the ability to forgive one another, themes which are also strong in the Pauline corpus. Matthew's portrayal of the teachings of Jesus calls to mind Hannah Arendt's illuminating account of the conditions of a public: the ability to make and keep promises, and the ability to forgive one another.[17] Matthew has a stronger sense than does Arendt of the continuity of tradition in the maintenance of communal life. This continuity is manifest in the accent on the irreversible authority of the Mosaic law. Yet Matthew's formal insistence on continuity is balanced by a substantive dramatization of the perfection of love as the central content of the law. Love captures the crucial themes: fidelity in commitments and mercy and forbearance. In Matthew's account love also challenges directly the pretensions of the means of violence.

4. Paul's account of Christian freedom enables us to appreciate the relativity of human cultures and social institutions. He opens the way to concrete processes of negotiating a common life among persons of diverse backgrounds and cultures. The logic of his position is to relativize social institutions as well, explicitly the household, but by implication, all institutional arrangements whatever. These structures can be accepted in their relativity and diversity for the sake of the ordered life they make possible. Still, they belong to the age which is passing away. Where ap-

propriate, they can be transformed in accord with the emerging freedom and community of the coming new age.

Paul's accent on the primacy of promise over law implies a repudiation of the formalistic elements in Matthew, though it becomes an alternative way of lifting up the centrality of love in building up a new kind of community. By the same token, Paul's attempt to transcend categories of law altogether in favor of the concrete dynamics of human interactions may underplay unduly the need for continuity and stability in human community. Concrete negotiations which are productive lead to results, results which become the touchstone for future interactions. These results properly take on the stability of law. In themselves they do not preclude radical openness toward new processes of negotiation as the occasion demands so long as their relativity and cultural contingency are specifically understood.

To oversimplify, Mark and Paul help us see the implications of eschatological existence for the household and its social role. Luke stimulates reflections in the economic realm; Matthew, in the political realm; and Paul, in the realm of culture, especially insofar as cultural forms order social interactions. Paul provides a general frame of reference for approaching all spheres of social life. What does not get raised is the possibility of eschatological existence when the relativity of the constitutive themes of Christian faith is itself understood, paving the way for interfaith negotiations of a qualitively new sort.

Short of the imaginative development for social institutions of themes integral to Christian understanding, a distinctively Christian ethic must confine itself to the challenges and opportunities of building up eschatological community. Social ethics would under those circumstances have to find other resources and methods for its inquiries, working in ways that are congruent with the basic institutions of modern society.

NOTES

1. I have elaborated these themes in *The Use of the Bible in Christian Ethics*. This book gives special attention to hermeneutical questions and spells out the underlying theological and philosophical assumptions of the essay.

2. The pertinent texts are numerous, but Romans 13 and 1 Pet. 2:13–17 are representative. Oscar Cullman's study, *The State in the New Testament* (New York: Charles Scribner's Sons, 1956), remains a solid account of explicit New Testament treatments of the state. The line of argument advanced in this chapter roughly parallels that proposed by Karl Barth in his tentative explorations of a possible political ethic. See his "The Christian Community and the Civil Community," in *Community, State, and Church: Three Essays* (Garden City, N.Y.: Doubleday & Co., 1960). On the primacy of eschatological community for Christian ethics, see James Cone, *God of the Oppressed* (New York: Seabury Press, 1975), 146–52, 206–17.

3. This characterization is most apt for the Gospel of Mark and the writings of Paul. Matthew and Luke moderate somewhat the intensity of the eschatological expectations found in these earlier materials. More strongly than Mark, Matthew reckons with the possibility that considerable time may pass before the kingdom of heaven is fully established. He maintains an orientation to that hoped-for event, but weighs more heavily daily concerns for the ordered life of developing communities of faith. In Luke-Acts, eschatology is taken up into a broad scheme of salvation history. The scheme has three sharply delineated periods: the period of law and prophets, the period of Jesus, and the period of the missionary expansion of the church. In one sense eschatology has for Luke been dissolved into the church's missionary expansion. Yet the epoch of the church is itself eschatological. It is the age of the Spirit, which is a new and decisive stage in historical development. In this respect, Luke shares the conviction of Mark and Paul that something qualitatively different is coming into being with Jesus and the Spirit-filled apostolate. Cf. Hans Conzelman, *The Theology of Luke*, Eng. trans. Geoffrey Buswell (New York: Harper and Brothers, 1960), 149–51.

4. It is easy for modern readers to underestimate the importance of these matters. After all, they concern ritual patterns with which most Christians feel little or no emotional involvement. Yet it is chiefly by way of shared rituals that we form a common world. If our world is enlarged to include those who are shaped by different social experiences, the most difficult problems we will face in learning to live together will concern ritual conflicts and misunderstandings. To tamper with cult and ritual is to tamper with deeply rooted human feelings and concerns.

5. Cf. Jacob Jervell, *Luke and the People of God, A New Look at Luke-Acts* (Minneapolis: Augsburg Publishing House, 1972), 145–46.

6. In introducing his discussion of the commands to love God and neighbor, the issue for Luke is not the determination of the greatest of the commandments. It concerns what one must do to inherit eternal life (Luke 10:25–28). Luke's Jesus condemns the Pharisees for scrupulously

tithing even herbs and spices while neglecting justice and the love of God. Yet he does not, like Matthew, refer to the latter as "weightier matters of the law" (cf. Matt. 23:23). The tithes ought to be paid, but without neglecting other obligations (Luke 11:42). In presenting Jesus' words about divorce Luke does not, as Mark, refer beyond Moses to a more elemental divine purpose (cf. Mark 10:1–12). Nor is the Mosaic Law portrayed as a concession to the hardness of human hearts. The prohibition of divorce is a straightforward and binding commandment of God (Luke 16:18). Finally, in narrating disputes about the sabbath—Luke reports four incidents: 6:1–5, 6–11; 13:10–17; 14:1–6—Jesus' position in each case accords with the law, such that the Jewish leaders are unable to sustain any objection to his words or deeds. At every point Luke presents Jesus as one who diligently observes the law and urges others to do so as well.

7. Cf. Luke T. Johnson, *The Literary Function of Possessions in Luke-Acts*, Society of Biblical Literature Dissertation Series 39 (Missoula, Mont.: Scholars Press, 1977).

8. John Howard Yoder, *The Politics of Jesus* (Grand Rapids, Mich.: Wm. B. Eerdman, 1972), 23.

9. Cf. Gerhard Barth, "Matthew's Understanding of the Law," in Gunther Bornkamm, Gerhard Barth, and Heinz Held, *Tradition and Interpretation in Matthew*, Eng. trans. Percy Scott (Philadelphia: Westminster Press, 1963), 75–76, 94.

10. The salient texts are all in the "sermon on the mount," Matt. 5:21–22, 27–28, 33–37; 6:1–18. The key text on radical vulnerability to adversaries is Matt. 5:38–48.

11. Cf. Hannah Arendt's claim that the bases for a public are the ability to make and keep promises and the ability to forgive one another, *The Human Condition* (Chicago: University of Chicago Press, 1958), 237.

12. Paul also contends that Jews who refuse the claims of the gospel may yet have a positive role to play in the divine economy. His view of this matter is not without ambiguity. "A hardening has come upon part of Israel," he notes, "until the full number of Gentiles come in" (Rom. 11:25). Why a "hardening"? How does Jewish unbelief help? Yet "all Israel will be saved," Paul adds (Rom. 11:26). "As regards the gospel," he continues, "they are enemies of God for your sake; but as regards election they are beloved for the sake of their forefathers. For the gifts and the call of God are irrevocable" (Rom. 11:28–29). Paul's insistence upon Israel's secure place in God's redemptive activity blunts any imperative to seek the conversion of Jews. It even establishes a frame of reference within which it is possible to affirm the continuing importance of the Jewish people for Christian understanding, and precisely in their Jewishness. Paul does not go so far, but his insight into the relativity of all human ways provides a matrix of understanding within which such a view might emerge.

13. Paul does on occasion speak of the law (*nomos*) of Christ, or of the law of the Spirit of life in Christ (e.g., Rom. 8:2). In such a usage, however, the term *nomos* does not refer to the ordering regulations of human life; it is not a functional equivalent to the Mosaic law. Rather, it designates something akin to an operative principle or fundamental dynamic. Thus, in Rom. 8, Paul is contrasting the dynamic at work in the Spirit of life in Jesus Christ with the dynamic at work in sin and death. He does not envision a new set of regulations and instructions derived from the Spirit of life in Christ which can order human affairs; not does he, like Matthew, offer a new interpretation of the law of Moses. He rather enunciates an altogether different basis for securing human life, dignity, worth, and wholeness with God. That new basis is promise, embracing freedom, love, and community in Christ.

14. This claim presupposes that the passages in 1 Cor. which speak of the subordination of women to men are not authentic Pauline passages (cf. 1 Cor. 11:3–16; 14:33b–36). For a discussion of the relevant considerations in this judgment, cf. Darrell J. Doughty, "Women and Liberation in the Churches of Paul and the Pauline Tradition," *The Drew Gateway* 50 (Winter, 1979): 7–8. The key points are three: the passages appear to be later insertions since they interrupt the flow of argument; they use language and modes of argument not characteristic of materials generally acknowledged to be authentically Pauline; and they contradict the explicit assertion in Gal. 3:28 of unity and equality among the sexes. My argument, however, does not depend upon the literary judgment that these texts are beyond doubt later insertions into the Pauline text. If Paul in fact wrote them, however, we face no small problem in displaying their coherence with the central thrust of undisputed Pauline texts and passages. Given the manifest power and originality of Paul's thought, it is at least somewhat implausible that he fell into blatant contradictions.

In general my own reading of New Testament texts accords with the interpretations of Elisabeth Schüssler Fiorenza, *In Memory of Her* (New York: Crossroad, 1983). Unfortunately, her work appeared after this study was completed.

15. This point does not hold for Deutero-Pauline materials nor for the Pastorals (cf. Col. 3:18–4:1, Eph. 5:22—6:8, 1 Tim. 2:8–15, 6:1–2, and Titus 2:1–10; cf. also 1 Pet. 2:13—3:7.

16. For a good discussion of the "haustafel," cf. James E. Crouch, *The Origin and Intention of the Colossian Haustafel* (Göttingen: Vandenhoeck & Ruprecht, 1972). I intend no general suggestion of "decline" in the movement from Pauline to Deutero-Pauline literature. Colossians and Ephesians are rich in insight and understanding, especially in the celebration of the cosmic significance of Christ and in the emphasis on the unifying power of the Christian gospel. The Pastorals contain no small amount of practical wisdom regarding the discipline necessary for

those who would exercise leadership in communities of faith. The point is simply that Paul's insight into the relativity of social structures is more radical and, I think, more profound than the attempts of the author of Ephesians to provide a christological legitimation and transformation of the patriarchal household. Paul's account of Christian freedom provides more room for the negotiation of cross-cultural community than do Deutero-Pauline interpretations of the gospel. See Schüssler Fiorenza, 226–35; 251–334.

17. Cf. Arendt, *Human Condition*, 237.

BIBLIOGRAPHY

Arendt, Hannah. *The Human Condition.* Chicago: University of Chicago Press, 1958.

Bachrach, Peter, and Morton Baratz. *Power and Poverty: Theory and Practice.* New York and London: Oxford University Press, 1970.

Barth, Karl. *Community, State, and Church: Three Essays.* Garden City, N.Y.: Doubleday & Co., 1960.

Bellah, Robert. *The Broken Covenant.* New York: Seabury Press, 1973.

Bentham, Jeremy. *An Introduction to the Principles of Morals and Legislation* (1789). Reprinted in *The English Philosophers from Bacon to Mill,* ed. Edwin A. Burtt. New York: Modern Library, 1939.

Berger, Peter L., and Thomas Luckmann. *The Social Construction of Reality: A Treatise in the Sociology of Knowledge.* Garden City, N.Y.: Doubleday, Anchor Books, 1967.

Bonhoeffer, Dietrich. *Life Together.* Eng. trans. John W. Doberstein. New York: Harper and Brothers, 1954.

Bornkamm, Gunther, Gerhard Barth, and Heinz Held. *Tradition and Interpretation in Matthew.* Eng. trans. Percy Scott. Philadelphia: Westminster Press, 1963.

Buber, Martin. *I and Thou.* Eng. trans. Ronald Gregor Smith. New York: Charles Scribner's Sons, 1958.

Cone, James. *God of the Oppressed.* New York: Seabury Press, 1975.

Conzelman, Hans. *The Theology of Luke.* Eng. trans. Geoffrey Buswell. Philadelphia: Fortress Press, 1982 (reprint).

Crossan, John Dominic, ed. *Paul Ricoeur on Biblical Hermeneutics.* Semeia 4. Missoula, Mont.: Scholars Press, 1975.

Crouch, James E. *The Origin and Intention of the Colossian Haustafel.* Göttingen: Vandenhoeck & Ruprecht, 1972.

Cullmann, Oscar. *The State in the New Testament.* New York: Charles Scribner's Sons, 1956.

Dubois, W. E. B. *The Souls of Black Folk* in *Three Negro Classics,* ed. John Hope Franklin. New York: Avon Books, 1965.

Gadamer, Hans-Georg. *Truth and Method*. Eng. trans. Garrett Barden and John Cumming. New York: Seabury Press, 1975.

Gouldner, Alvin W. *The Coming Crisis of Western Sociology*. New York: Basic Books, 1970.

Gustafson, James M. *Can Ethics Be Christian?* Chicago: University of Chicago Press, 1975.

———. *Christ and the Moral Life*. New York: Harper & Row, 1968.

———. *Christian Ethics and the Community*. Philadelphia: Pilgrim Press, 1971.

———. *The Contributions of Theology to Medical Ethics*. Milwaukee: Marquette University Press, 1975.

Habermas, Juergen. *Communication and the Evolution of Society*. Eng. Trans. Thomas McCarthy. Boston: Beacon Press, 1976.

———. *Legitimation Crisis*. Eng. trans. Thomas McCarthy. Boston: Beacon Press, 1973.

Hauerwas, Stanley. *Truthfulness and Tragedy: Further Investigations in Christian Ethics*. Notre Dame: Ind.: University of Notre Dame Press, 1977.

Harrod, Howard L. *The Human Center: Moral Agency in the Social World*. Philadelphia: Fortress Press, 1981.

Hegel, G. F. W. *The Phenomenology of Mind*. Eng. trans. J. B. Baillie. London: George Allen & Unwin, 1931.

Heidegger, Martin. *Being and Time*. Eng. trans. John Macquarrie and Edward Robinson. London: SCM Press, 1962.

———. "Letter on Humanism" in *Philosophy in the Twentieth Century: An Anthology*, eds. William Barrett and Henry D. Aiken. Vol. III. New York: Random House, 1962.

———. *On Time and Being*. Eng. trans. Joan Stambaugh. New York: Harper & Row, 1972.

Husserl, Edmund. *Cartesian Meditations: An Introduction to Phenomenology*. Eng. trans. Dorion Cairns. The Hague: Martinus Nijhoff, 1960.

———. *The Crisis of European Sciences and Transcendental Phenomenology: An Introduction to Phenomenological Philosophy*. Eng. Trans. David Carr. Evanston, Ill.: Northwestern University Press, 1970.

———. "Phenomenology." Eng. trans. Richard E. Palmer. *Encyclopaedia Britannica* (1927).

Jervell, Jacob. *Luke and the People of God: A New Look at Luke-Acts*. Minneapolis: Augsburg Pub. House, 1972.

Johnson, Chalmers. *Revolutionary Change*. Boston: Little, Brown & Company, 1966.

Johnson, Luke T. *The Literary Function of Possessions in Luke-Acts*. *SBL Dissertation Series 39*. Missoula, Mont.: Scholars Press, 1977.

Kant, Immanuel. *Critique of Practical Reason*. Eng. trans. Lewis White Beck. New York: Bobbs-Merrill, Library of Liberal Acts, 1956.

Kant, Immanuel. *Fundamental Principles of the Metaphysic of Morals.* Eng. Trans. Thomas K. Abbott. Indianapolis: Bobbs-Merrill, Library of Liberal Arts, 1949.

Kierkegaard, Søren. *Philosophical Fragments.* Eng. trans. David F. Swenson. Princeton: Princeton University Press, 1936.

Levinas, Immanuel. *Totality and Infinity: An Essay on Exteriority.* Eng. Trans. Alphonso Lingis. Pittsburgh: Duquesne University Press, 1969.

Little, H. Ganse. *Decision and Responsibility: A Wrinkle in Time.* Missoula, Mont.: Scholars Press, 1974.

Lukes, Steven. *Power: A Radical View.* London: MacMillan & Co., 1974.

Marx, Karl. *Economic and Philosophical Manuscripts of 1844.* New York: International Publishers, 1964.

McRae. Duncan, Jr. *The Social Function of Social Science.* New Haven, Conn.: Yale University Press, 1976.

Mead, G. H. *Mind, Self, and Society.* Chicago: University of Chicago Press, 1934.

Merleau-Ponty, Maurice. *The Primacy of Perception,* ed. James M. Edie. Evanston, Ill.: Northwestern University Press, 1964.

Nabert, Jean. *Le Désir de Dieu.* Paris: Aubier, 1966.

———. *Elements for an Ethic.* Eng. Trans. William J. Petrek. Evanston, Ill.: Northwestern University Press, 1969.

Niebuhr, H. Richard. *Radical Monotheism and Western Culture.* New York: Harper & Row, 1960.

———. *The Responsible Self: An Essay in Christian Moral Philosophy.* New York: Harper & Row, 1963.

Nietzsche, Friedrich. *The Genealogy of Morals.* Eng. trans. Francis Golffing. Garden City, N.Y.: Doubleday Anchor Books, 1956.

Ogletree, Thomas W. *The Use of the Bible in Christian Ethics: A Constructive Essay.* Philadelphia: Fortress Press, 1983; Oxford: Basil Blackwell, 1984.

Parsons, Talcott. *Politics and Social Structure.* New York: Free Press, 1969.

Parsons, Talcott, and Edward Shils, eds. *Toward a General Theory of Action.* New York: Harper & Row, 1962.

Ramsey, Paul. *Basic Christian Ethics.* New York: Charles Scribner's Sons, 1950.

———. *The Ethics of Fetal Research.* New Haven, Conn.: Yale University Press, 1975.

———. *The Just War: Force and Political Responsibility.* New York: Charles Scribner's Sons, 1968.

Rawls, John. *A Theory of Justice.* Cambridge, Mass.: Harvard University Press, 1971.

Ricoeur, Paul. *Fallible Man.* Eng. trans. Charles Kelbley. Chicago: Henry Regnery, 1965.

————. *Freedom and Nature: The Voluntary and the Involuntary.* Eng. trans. Erazim V. Kohák. Evanston, Ill.: Northwestern University Press, 1966.

————. *Freud and Philosophy: An Essay on Interpretation.* Eng. trans. Denis Savage. New Haven, Conn.: Yale University Press, 1970.

————. *Interpretation Theory: Discourse and the Surplus of Meaning.* Forth Worth, Tex.: Texas Christian University Press, 1976.

————. *Philosophie de la Volonté: Le Volontaire et L'Involontaire.* Paris: Aubier, Éditions Montaigne, 1950.

————. *Philosophie de la Volonté: Finitude et Culpabilité.* Vol. I. *L'Homme Fallible.* Paris: Aubier, Éditions Montaigne, 1960.

————. *Symbolism of Evil.* Eng. trans. Emerson Buchanan. Boston: Beacon Press, 1969.

Sartre, Jean-Paul. *Being and Nothingness.* Eng. trans. Hazel E. Barnes. New York: Philosophical Library, 1956.

————. *Critique de la Raison Dialectique: Précédé de Question de Methode.* Paris: Gallimard, 1960.

Scheler, Max. *Formalism in Ethics and Non-Formal Ethics of Values.* Eng. trans. Manfred S. Frings and Roger L. Funk. Evanston, Ill.: Northwestern University Press, 1973.

Schüssler Fiorenza, Elisabeth. *In Memory of Her: A Feminist Theological Reconstruction of Christian Origins.* New York: Crossroad, 1983.

Schutz, Alfred. *Collected Papers.* Vol. I. *The Problem of Social Reality.* The Hague: Martinus Nijhoff, 1967.

Schutz, Alfred, and Thomas Luckmann. *The Structures of the Life-World.* Eng. trans. Richard M. Zaner and H. Tristram Engelhardt, Jr. Evanston, Ill.: Northwestern University Press, 1973.

James Sellers. *Public Ethics.* New York: MacMillan Co., 1970.

Tillich, Paul. *Love, Power and Justice.* New York: Oxford University Press, 1954.

————. *Systematic Theology.* Vol. III. *Life and the Spirit, History and the Kingdom of God.* Chicago: University of Chicago Press, 1963.

Tracy, David. *The Analogical Imagination: Christian Theology and the Culture of Pluralism.* New York: Crossroad, 1981.

Winter, Gibson. *Being Free: Reflections on America's Cultural Revolution.* New York: MacMillan Co., 1966.

————. *Elements for a Social Ethic: Scientific and Ethical Perspectives on Social Process.* New York: MacMillan Co., 1966.

Yoder, John Howard. *The Politics of Jesus.* Grand Rapids: Wm. B. Eerdmans, 1972.

Zaner, Richard. *The Problem of Embodiment: Some Contributions to a Phenomenology of the Body.* The Hague: Martinus Nijhoff, 1971.

SUBJECT INDEX

AUTHOR INDEX

Arendt, Hannah, 144, 147 n. 11,
149 n. 17
Aristotle, 22

Bachrach, Peter, 34 n. 27
Baratz, Morton, 34 n. 27
Barth, Gerhard, 147 n. 9
Barth, Karl, 146 n. 2
Bellah, Robert, 125 n. 48
Bentham, Jeremy, 13, 31 n. 8
Berger, Peter, 32 n. 14
Bonhoeffer, Dietrich, 44, 61 n.
16
Buber, Martin, 92 n. 21

Childress, James, 124 n. 17
Christ, Carol, 8 n. 5
Conzelmann, Hans, 146 n. 3
Crites, Stephen, 60 n. 14
Crouch, James E., 148 n. 16
Cullmann, Oscar, 146 n. 2

Doughty, Darrell J., 148 n. 14
Dubois, W. E. B., 125–26 n. 51

Erikson, Erik H., 63 n. 35

Freud, Sigmund, 117

Gadamer, Hans-Georg, 1, 8 n. 1,
29, 33 n. 26, 114, 119, 120,
122, 125 nn. 39, 50, 126 n. 52

Gouldner, Alvin W., 34 n. 27,
80
Gustafson, James M., 103–4,
123 nn. 11, 12, 13, 14

Habermas, Jürgen, 32–33 n. 16,
33 n. 27
Harrod, Howard L., 32 n. 12,
124 n. 28
Hauerwas, Stanley, 122, 123 nn.
14, 15, 124 n. 21
Hegel, G. F. W., 120, 125 n. 51
Heidegger, Martin, 16, 23–24,
32 n. 11, 33 nn. 20, 21, 22, 80,
113, 114, 124 n. 25, 125 nn.
38, 40, 41
Hobbes, Thomas, 44
Hume, David, 107
Husserl, Edmund, 15, 16, 31 n.
9, 32 n. 10, 33 n. 18, 45, 59 n.
1, 61 n. 19, 81, 95 n. 26, 99,
106, 107, 110, 112, 124 nn.
22, 23, 25, 27

Jervell, Jacob, 146 n. 5
Johnson, Chalmers, 60 n. 6
Johnson, Luke T., 147 n. 7

Kant, Immanuel, 12–13, 14, 25,
31 nn. 4, 5, 6, 7, 49, 62 n. 27,

161